Natural Houses
The Residential Architecture of Andersson-Wise

Arthur Andersson and Chris Wise

Princeton Architectural Press
New York

Published by
Princeton Architectural Press
37 East Seventh Street
New York, New York 10003

For a free catalog of books, call 1-800-722-6657.
Visit our website at www.papress.com.

© 2010 Princeton Architectural Press
All rights reserved
Printed and bound in China
13 12 11 10   1 2 3 4   First edition

No part of this book may be used or reproduced in any manner without written permission from the publisher, except in the context of reviews.

Every reasonable attempt has been made to identify owners of copyright. Errors or omissions will be corrected in subsequent editions.

Initial project descriptions: Julien Devereux
Editor: Wendy Fuller
Designer: Jan Haux

Special thanks to: Nettie Aljian, Bree Anne Apperley, Sara Bader, Nicola Bednarek, Janet Behning, Becca Casbon, Carina Cha, Tom Cho, Penny (Yuen Pik) Chu, Russell Fernandez, Pete Fitzpatrick, Erin Kim, Nancy Eklund Later, Linda Lee, Laurie Manfra, John Myers, Katharine Myers, Dan Simon, Andrew Stepanian, Jennifer Thompson, Paul Wagner, Joseph Weston, and Deb Wood of Princeton Architectural Press
—Kevin C. Lippert, publisher

Library of Congress Cataloging-in-Publication Data
Andersson, Arthur, 1957–
 Natural houses : the residential architecture of Andersson-Wise / Arthur Andersson and Chris Wise. — 1st ed.
    p. cm.
 ISBN 978-1-56898-879-5 (alk. paper)
 1.  Andersson-Wise. 2.  Architecture, Domestic—United States. I. Wise, Chris, 1964– II. Title.
 NA737.A55A4 2010
 728—dc22
                    2009015316

Contents

| | |
|---|---|
| 10 | Preface |
| 12 | Introduction |
| | by Rick Sundberg |
| 14 | Tower House |
| 30 | Lake House |
| 46 | Super Natural |
| | by Jen Renzi |
| 58 | House Above Lake Austin |
| 76 | Stone Creek Camp |
| 108 | On the Salubrity of Sites |
| | by Frederick Steiner |
| 116 | Collector's House |
| 132 | Temple Ranch |
| 152 | Cabin on Flathead Lake |
| 174 | Influential Texts |
| 175 | Illustration Credits |
| 176 | Project Team Credits |

Preface

The projects in this book were designed in our studio in Austin, Texas, from 2000 to 2008. Five of the seven shown are located in and around Austin, where the climate is temperate but hot, and most years the warm months of summer stretch all the way to Thanksgiving. The other two projects are located in far northern Montana, where protection from the cold is its own kind of celebration.

Our studio is made up of a close group of designers and architects. Conversation and dialogue about the work is our daily bread. This collaborative spirit opens us to many influences—visual, musical, and literary. On any given day, discussing the impact of a decision will bring us back to the eloquent phrase of Sir Winston Churchill: "We shape our buildings; thereafter they shape us." This is an aphorism that applies to all of what we do.

Our particular architecture is shaped not so much by us but by its place. By this we mean climate, site geology, and site biology: sun, wind, temperature, terrain, structure, orientation—the things that grow and that can grow there. These elements beckon our engagement and ask for interpretation. We have discovered that experiences brought on by nature—sunlight moving through composed space and onto surfaces; emotional strength gained in a protected space while looking out to a wild one; grand vistas enjoyed in the presence of intimate rooms—these are the gifts nature has given. We aspire to connect intimately with the places in which we build. We view our buildings, and the experience of inhabiting them, as celebrations of those places.

We have been fortunate to share the process of making these buildings with inspired and energetic colleagues. A team of people works on each project, in some cases for several years, to achieve a desired result. Special thanks to Andersson-Wise Architects' current staff including: Robin Bagley, Jesse Coleman, Catherine Craig, Travis Greig, Trish Laird, Jill Reinecke-Clark, Christopher Sanders, and Leland Ulmer. Also a special thanks to John E. van Duyl, Peggy Hamilton Houser, Nancy Eklund Later, Wendy Fuller, Art Gray, Matthew Millman, Paul Bardagjy, and Peter Williams for their assistance in making this book a reality. Finally, additional thanks go to Matthew Ames, Susan Benz, Gregory Brooks, Xavier Cantu, Anita Chumnanvech, Erlene Clark, Tim Dacey, Steven Dvorak, Daniel Gruber, Kristen Heaney, Wenny Hsu, Becky Joye, Alexis Kanter, Alexandra Lopez, Laura McQuary,

Vincent Moccia, James Moore, and all former studio colleagues for their contributions.

We thank each of our clients who must know that we treasure the memories as well as the friendships that have grown out of our mutual efforts.

Finally, we appreciate the influences of other architects, artisans, and artists with whom we have had the honor of working. We have learned much by watching others who excel at their craft. Both of us practiced closely with Charles Moore, an architect who always reminded us that buildings are for people, not for the record books. This humanist approach has stayed with us and will continue to guide our work.

>    Arthur Andersson
>    Chris Wise
>    Austin, Texas

Introduction
The Architecture of Andersson-Wise
Rick Sundberg

The architecture of Andersson-Wise addresses the tension between nature and the built environment—calling into question what we consider natural. At Stone Creek Camp, the intersection of two types of space—the manmade shelter and the surrounding wilderness—provides an opportunity for reflection. By influencing our senses, the building elevates our understanding of the landscape, giving it a historical and aesthetic meaning.

The built environment of the Montana Camp interacts with nature in seemingly endless ways. Wood, stone, and grasses form the buildings and the landscape around them, erasing distinctions. Inside the buildings, you find yourself literally in nature. Decks and deeply screened porches provide in-between places, offering both prospect and refuge. The paths between buildings, which take you through meadows and down alleys, encourage you to encounter buildings from a diagonal, rather than on an axial orientation.

Arthur Andersson and Chris Wise's firm owes much to the legacy of Charles Moore, an intuitive humanist, architect, and planner whose greatest legacy was his exploration of place and its representation. His work incited responses from all the senses. Andersson-Wise internalized these lessons, and their work has a similar strength in the way it engages us.

In his book *The Eyes of the Skin*, Finnish architect Juhani Pallasmaa writes: "The eye is the organ of separation and distance, whereas touch is the sense of nearness, intimacy, and affection." The Montana Camp engages both our senses of sight and touch, though not in ways we might expect.

Our visual perception of the site is quietly manipulated, setting the architecture in motion. Buildings cantilever over the site, or burrow into it. The experience shifts from floating over the ground—contemplating a layered foreground with a distant horizon of the Rockies—to peering out an at-grade window, a literal view of the ground.

Tactility, expressed through an eloquence of craft, the use of textured materials, and the logical expression of structural systems, gives the buildings a rightness within the landscape. They belong there, both materially and historically. The use of wood, stone, and earth reinterpret the sod house and log cabin. The materials play with us. The heavy materiality of the master suite's facade—basically firewood—floats above the landscape, held together by a steel frame. By taking the rough material object and organizing it, the wood wall does something unexpected. Texture—a sense that one usually experiences by touch—becomes instead something that one experiences through sight, as a compositional element.

Experiencing the project through the senses evokes something almost semiconscious, perhaps genetic, in us. It is a natural place.

Tower House
Leander, Texas, 2008

Of the series of Highland Lakes that terrace the hill country to the west of Austin, Lake Travis is the longest, winding over sixty miles through the natural terrain.

There are a few small limestone cabins from the 1930s on Lake Travis, used primarily in the summer. One such cabin sits on a slope rising from the water under a canopy of native oak and cedar trees. It had one large room, a little sleeping room, a kitchen, and a porch facing the water. Our clients requested two additional bedrooms with baths and a living area for larger groups to gather in. Rather than add onto the old cabin, we chose to open it up inside and locate the new sleeping quarters in a separate building.

The stone cabin is now juxtaposed with a vertical tower of wood, rising up out of the forest and into the bright Texas sky. The Tower draws you in to see the lake, barely visible at ground level through the thickets of trees.

Upon entering the Tower House, a small arrival space leads to shaded stairs inserted between the outside wall and the interior rooms. As you walk up, rectangular openings in the exterior wall invite breezes to circulate and offer brief, tantalizing glimpses of trees, sky, and lake. The orientation changes on every floor due to the winding nature of the stair and circulation path. Walking is the best way to experience the building, but a small elevator is also available for direct transport to the top.

Two small bedrooms with bathrooms occupy the first and second floors. The interior walls are made of birch plywood, which is lighter in tone than the Massaranduba wood outside. Large corner windows within each of the bedrooms reveal broad views of the woods and the lake. Finally, above the bedroom spaces, a third level opens to a panorama of the lake and distant rolling hills beyond. On this terrace, some thirty feet above the ground, even the hottest summer afternoon is enjoyed under a roof open to the prevailing breezes blowing from the lake. In the tower, site and orientation provide natural air cooling without relying on an air conditioning system.

View of Tower House from courtyard looking west

View of Tower House entrance from courtyard

(clockwise from top):
View of existing lodge and Tower House looking south
Slatted opening detail
Detail of east facade

1 Renovated lodge
2 Tower House

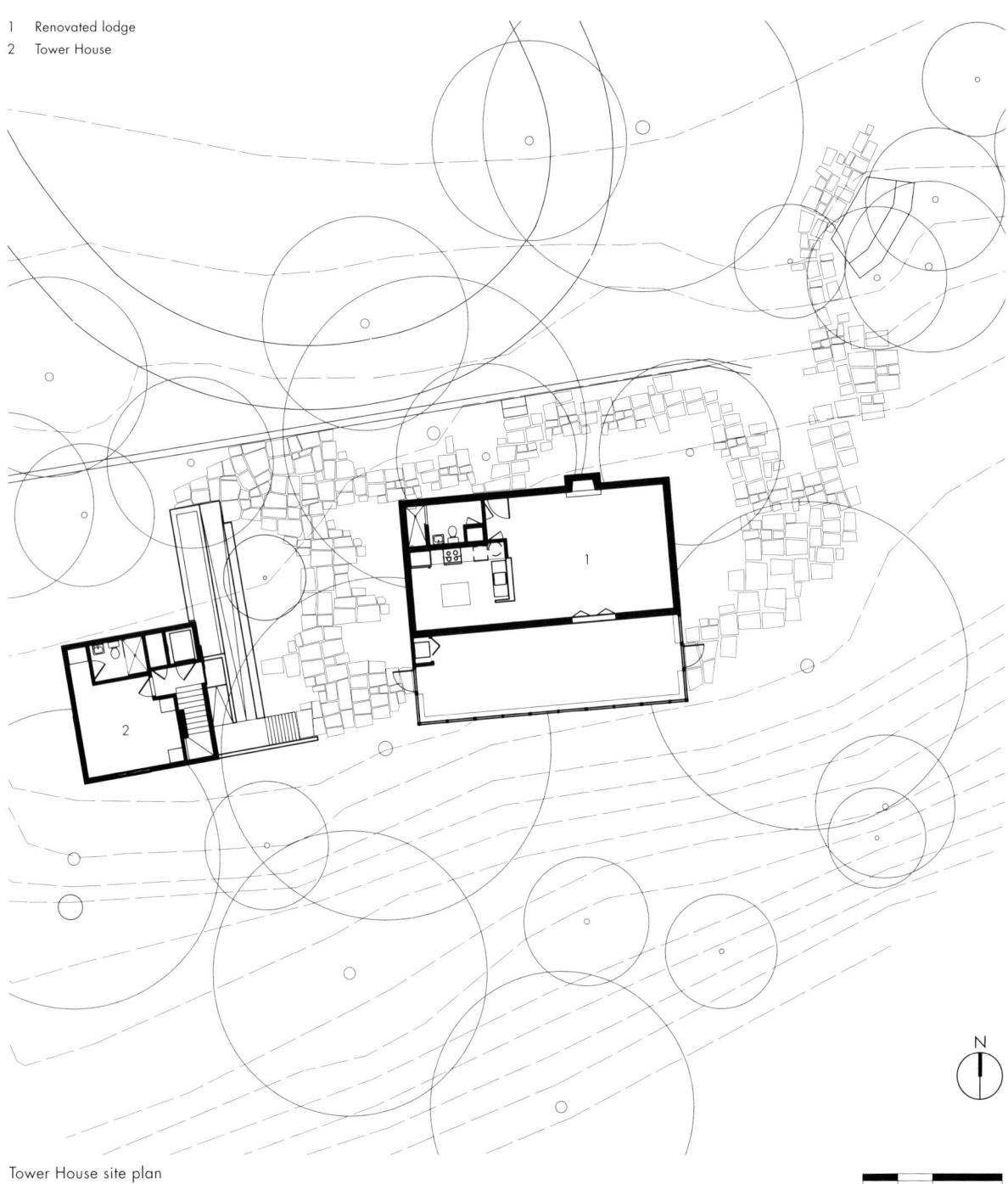

Tower House site plan

Tower House north facade

(counterclockwise from top):
View of lake at second-floor landing
Corner detail of tower roof
View of slatted opening detail from stair

opposite:
Balcony at second-floor landing

overleaf:
View of lake from balcony

(clockwise from top):
Second-floor bedroom
Second-floor bathroom
Barn door to bathroom on second floor

opposite:
Custom bed detail

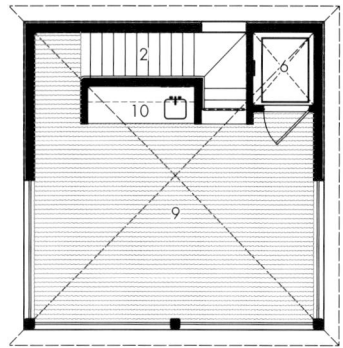

Third-floor plan

1. Entry
2. Stair
3. Master bedroom
4. Bathroom
5. Machine room
6. Elevator
7. Landing
8. Bedroom
9. Roof terrace
10. Kitchenette

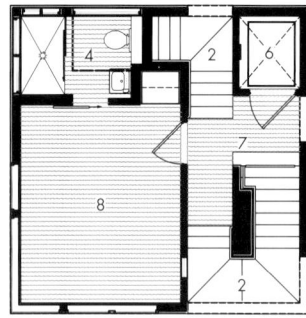

Second-floor plan

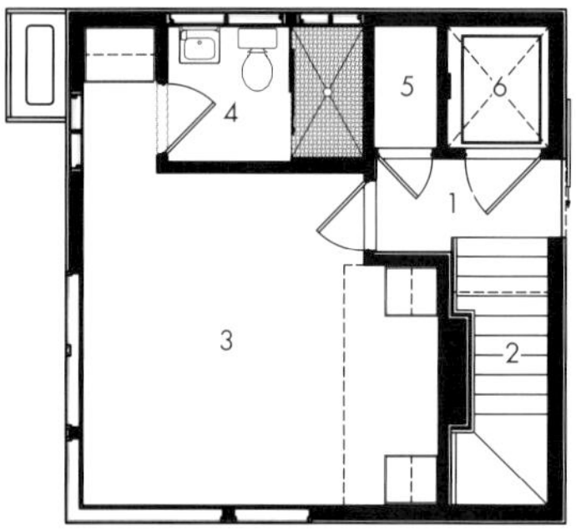

Tower House ground-floor plan

1. Exterior Stair
2. Elevator
3. Roof terrace

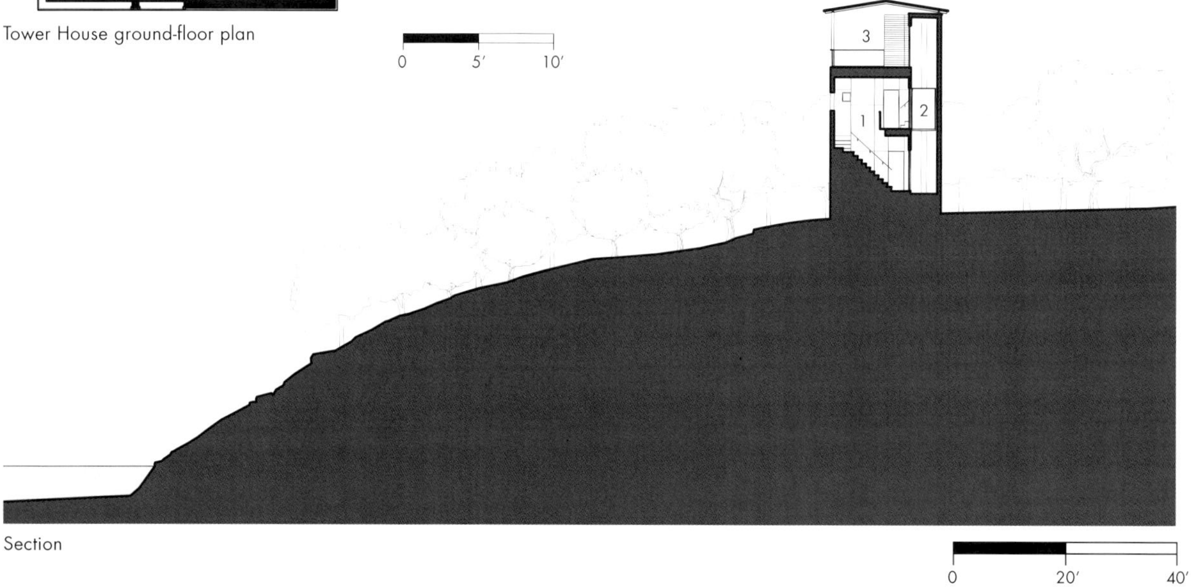

Section

26　Natural Houses

Corner window detail on second floor

(top to bottom):
Terrace view looking west
Terrace view looking south

View of Tower House from Lake Travis

Lake House
Austin, Texas, 2002

This structure, located on the steeply sloped bank of Lake Austin, is designed for downtime. A nearly mile-long path leads the visitor down the hill, over a suspension bridge constructed of individual segments strung onto cables that spans a ravine, and finally down to the boat house. The simple, elegant building rises above the water, resting on the surface like a water skater. And like the surface-skimming insect, this off-the-grid domicile exerts a minimal impact on its surroundings. Its structure, fabricated into a single framework of steel and barged to the site, is anchored into rock beneath the water. A floating carpenter shop was used to complete the construction from the water side.

Breezes from the lake-top enter and exit through screens, allowing the living spaces to breathe along with the river valley. The wind and water combine to provide natural cooling for the entire structure. On the north and east sides, the lower screens swing out to create full-height openings that are impromptu diving platforms.

The Lake House provides a respite from the exhaustions of heat and the exertion of swimming, but it constantly reminds occupants of their proximity.

View of east facade from Lake Austin

(clockwise from top):
View from hilltop path
Stair to screened room
Bridge to screened room

Bridge to shoal

overleaf:
View of west facade

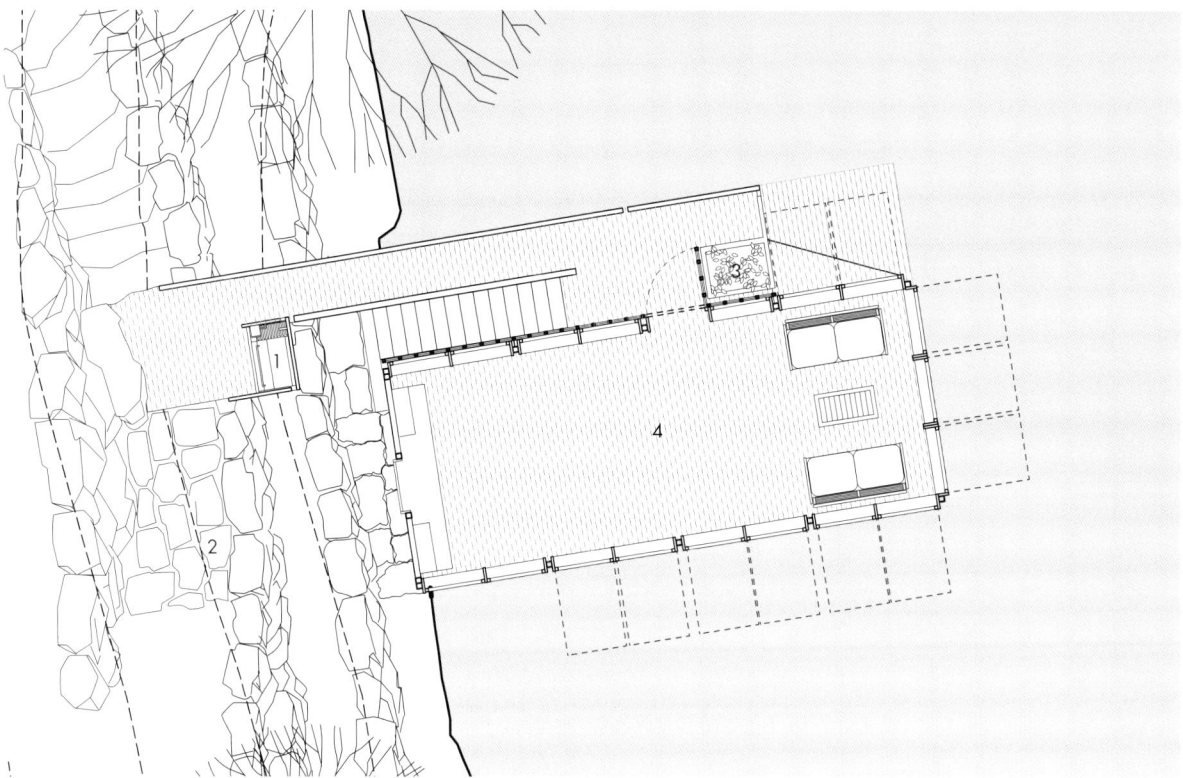

Porch plan

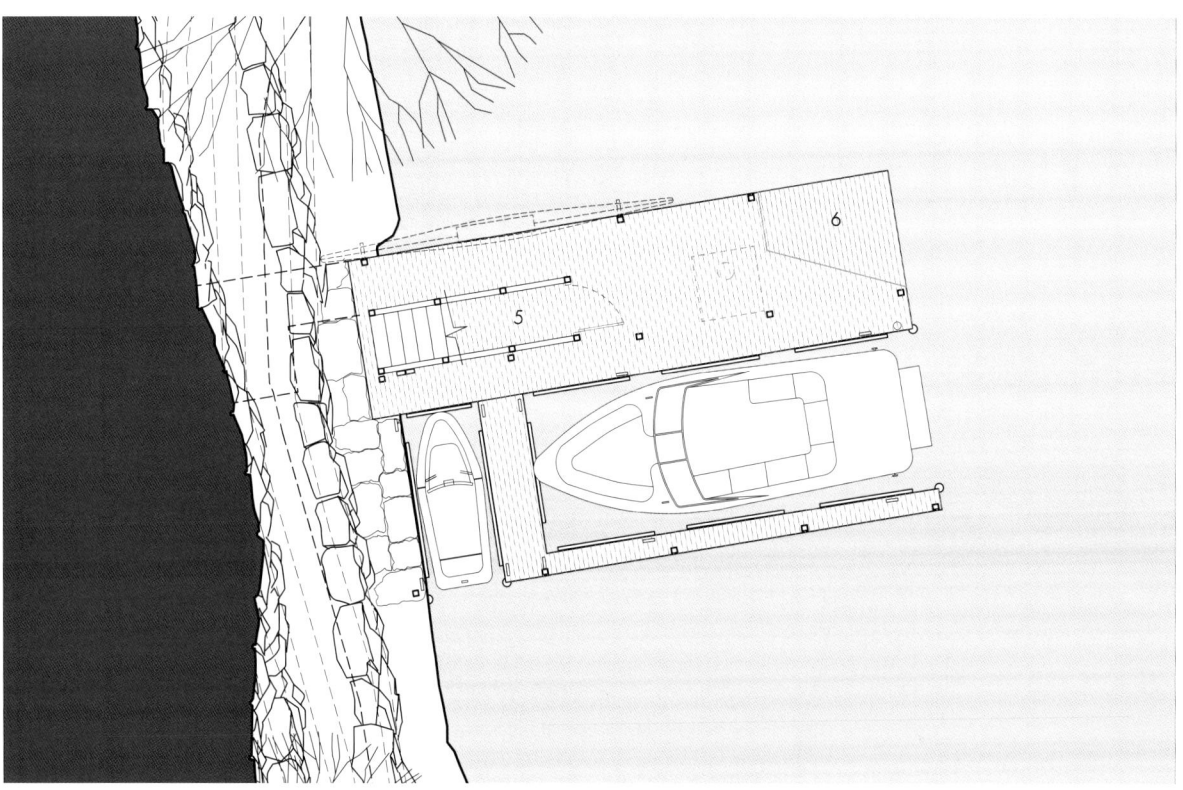

Lake House boat dock plan

1 Grill
2 Patio
3 Planter
4 Screened porch
5 Storage
6 Sculling dock

South facade

(counterclockwise from top):
South facade detail
Lantern shelf detail
Shower at boat slip

opposite:
South facade detail

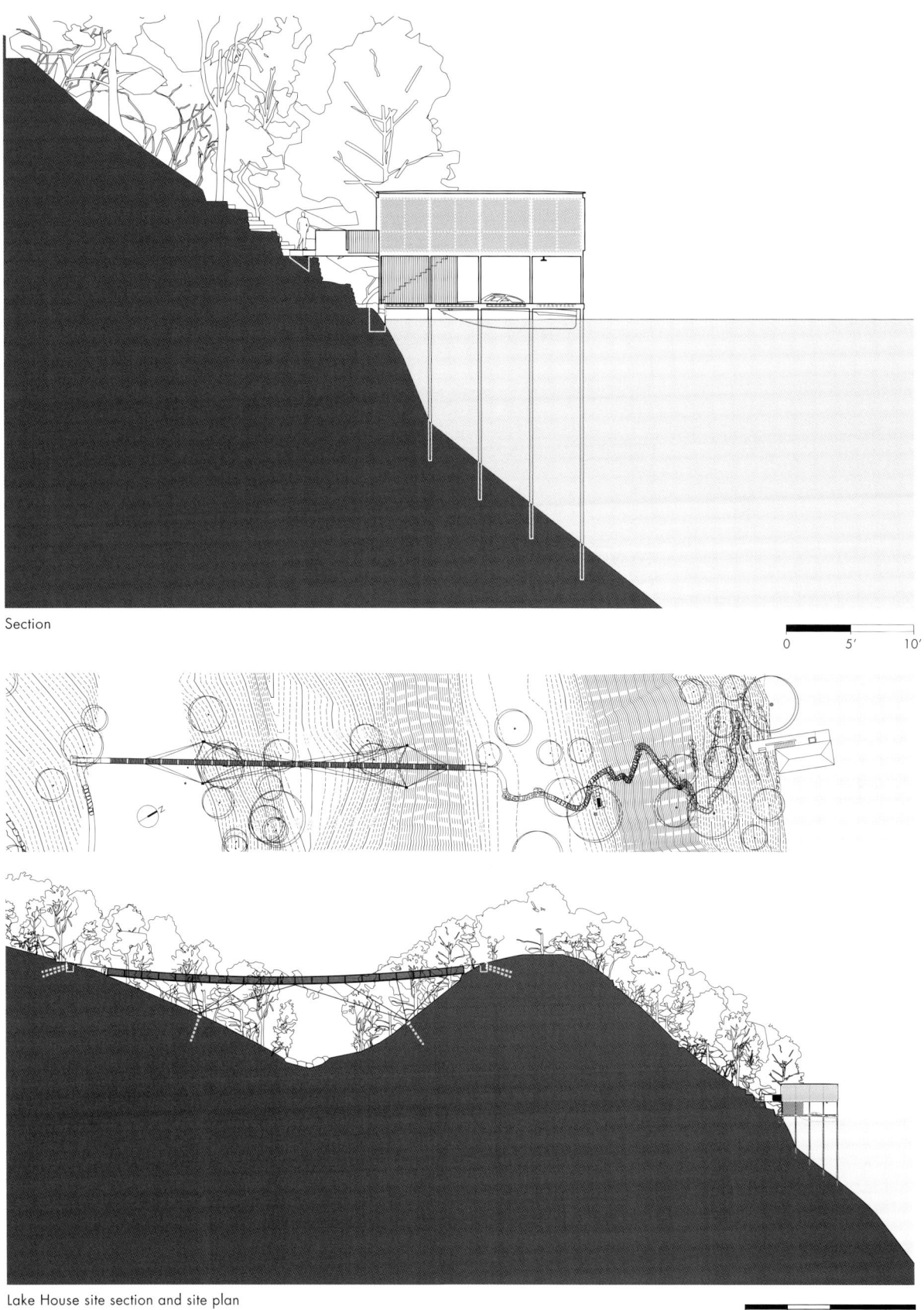

Section

Lake House site section and site plan

North facade

Open screens

(clockwise from top):
Suspension bridge to Lake House
East facade
Hanging basket detail at suspension bridge

(counterclockwise from top):
View from Lake Austin
Screened room
Screened room detail

opposite:
Screened room detail

Super Natural

Jen Renzi

The first thing the visitor notices about an Andersson-Wise design—whether a home or a church or an art museum—is the light. A small aperture cut into a thick stone wall coaxes the sunrise in for a fleeting hour each morning. Windows screened by wood slats slice daylight into a Donald Judd-like geometry. A covered porch curtained in white hemp glows like the inside of a Noguchi lantern in the late-afternoon glare. Dusk hits a chunk of onyx on a high steel ledge and fractures into a kaleidoscopic shimmer. In the hands of Arthur Andersson and Chris Wise, light is ethereal, mysterious, slippery, strange, and transcendent.

 It's no wonder that the two have carved out a niche in ecclesiastical design; their handling of illumination verges on the spiritual. Credit this to Wise's upbringing. "My dad was a minister, and we lived right next door to the church," he says. "I grew up sneaking into sanctuaries. Quite early in life, I had an epiphany about how light interacts with space—and how spatial complexity can create poetic effects." He observed how, as sunlight shifted from hour to hour and season to season, architecture became a living, breathing organism.

 The two likewise use daylight as a building material. Andersson and Wise have a soft spot for light-catchers, clerestories, and three-sided dormers that grab sunlight from different directions throughout the day. Thick facades are often punctured with "spirit" windows—their term for small apertures that mold light into luminous planes, like miniature Dan Flavin installations. "We explore ways of bending light and threading it through a building, from one end to the other," Andersson explains. That pathway is often oblique. They use walls as mirrors to bounce illumination, extending its reach while softening its harshness. In renovating the Austin home of an art collector, for instance, the duo baffled a series of existing skylights by installing drop ceilings below—not unlike shallow trays placed to catch a water leak. Now, instead of blasting in from overhead, the daylight spills gracefully over the edges like a waterfall, making a previously uninhabitable space serene.

 Tempering sunlight is of course crucial in Austin, the firm's home base. During the summer especially—and it feels like summer much of the year—there is nothing subtle or coy about the light. It is hard core. You are constantly seeking refuge from it, sniffing out the elusive shade like a truffle hunter. Sure, the heat can seem comforting at first, even a bit luxuriant, like a sauna. But the moment your defenses drop and your muscles loosen, the heat bores down into your soul and holds you in its fast grip. The sun is a cruel tease: it burns everything into bright, white focus then forces your eyes to shut tight against it. In Austin, nature can be extreme and often harsh.

Andersson-Wise is a product of this environment. The firm's work shows Mother Earth for what she is: beautiful, yes, but also fearsome. The siting of their buildings highlights the more rugged—even treacherous—aspects of the surrounding landscape. A two-hundred-foot cable-stay suspension bridge arcs precariously across a deep ravine. Houses engage with steep cliffs, perch on vertiginous precipices, cantilever into thin air, or nestle into treetops. Note the cabin on Flathead Lake, which—with its angled roofline and stilt-like base—recalls a butterfly specimen, pinned almost invisibly to its support. You would be forgiven for thinking that this avian structure might flutter off into the forest. And the architects answered one client's request for a low-slung ranch house with a modernist, three-story tower—a lighthouse, really—that offers dizzying views of a lake one hundred feet below. "Spaces like this get your adrenaline pumping a little bit," Andersson emphasizes.

These structures have a thrill-seeking side that belies an otherwise composed bearing—a characteristic shared with their creators. While Wise was sneaking into churches, Andersson spent his formative years taking in the great outdoors. An itinerant upbringing took him from Los Angeles to Alaska to Denver, environments where vermillion sunsets, craggy peaks, and never-ending horizon lines instilled a sense of awe and exhilaration that fuels his creativity. "As a result of moving around so much at a young age, I've always drawn strength from the environment," he explains.

Andersson is inspired by writers and artists who likewise take nature as muse, from Henry David Thoreau and Ralph Waldo Emerson to the Hudson River school painters. He finds a kindred spirit in Thomas Cole's majestic thunderstorms, Albert Bierstadt's Wild West, and the psychologically charged imagery of German romanticist Caspar David Friedrich, known for isolating solo figures against overwhelming landscapes. "Their paintings share a common quality, capturing the spirit of the pioneer—out on your own, pushing the boundaries," says Andersson. "Tapping into that sense of adventure fuels our practice."

The firm's designs certainly push boundaries, but not always on the surface. Their buildings are not self-consciously avant-garde in appearance, nor do they grandstand. Most are planar, precise, and cool—characteristics that usually connote restfulness, not risk taking. Forms are often derived from the American vernacular of barns and cottages, with elemental, Monopoly-piece shapes and angled rooflines. Many are sided in crisp slats of Douglas fir or Massaranduba, which lend an almost traditional bearing. "We make dramatic things," says Wise. "But they don't always manifest themselves in overtly dramatic ways."

Not outwardly, perhaps. Inside, though, is another matter entirely. What appears from the outside to be a meditative space will, more often than not, make your jaw drop and your pulse race. Walls of full-height glass melt away, forcing your gaze out to the landscape beyond. Looking through, you slip into a mysterious place where you're simultaneously at one with the elements and aware of the need for protection from such overwhelming forces. It's a funny mental trick: making you conscious of the innate human need for comfort, and thus demanding a heightened awareness (and greater appreciation) of your architectural surroundings. In this way, the designers draw attention to their work by diverting it to something else. Such spaces pay homage to Immanuel Kant's distinction between the fleeting nature of one-note beauty and the more enduring splendor of the sublime. "Beauty alone doesn't hold your interest for very long," says Andersson. "You want things to be a little…scary. But the kind of awe that derives from nature is extraordinarily tranquil."

Take Andersson-Wise's design of Stone Creek Camp in Bigfork, Montana, a rural retreat for a Tucson-based couple. Spread over fifteen acres, the getaway comprises eight structures alighting a steep slope: a gatehouse, main residence, guest cottage, communal lodge, a pair of docks (one for boats, one for swimming), and the property's original cabin. The site overlooks Flathead Lake, an expansive, glassy surface that reflects its verdant environs. "The lake is very powerful," says Andersson. "Even when you can't see it, you sense it." The largest freshwater lake west of the Mississippi River, it is thirty-two miles long and fifteen wide—which translates to a lot of open sky. "The light in Montana stops you in your tracks. At twilight, misty clouds blow across the lake and everything blooms pink."

A project of such scope put Andersson-Wise's institutional background to good use. Here, they sketched out a master plan to make individual buildings seem connected but still private, so the compound feels like an integrated village. "Each is designed like a geode: thick and solid on one side and open on the other," Andersson explains. The "thick" sides, with fewer and smaller windows, face up the hill, ensuring that buildings further up the slope can't see in. And, more importantly, that their lake view—the "open" side—is not compromised by bright lights below.

The various structures are arranged to take advantage of natural clearings, avoid razing trees, and leave flowing rivulets undisturbed. Passive solar strategies help reduce the drain on heating, air conditioning, and other mechanical systems. Windows, for instance, are positioned to take advantage of shade and cross breezes in the summer and suck in warmth in cooler months. "We have designed environmentally conscientious buildings from the outset," notes Andersson. Nature is a muse, but she is also a force to be respected.

One enters the property via a two-part gatehouse capped by a butterfly roof. The barn—which houses a garage, mechanical equipment, and a workroom—is clad in ebony-stained wood siding that melds into the landscape. Steps lead down to the lodge—actually a cluster of three buildings sheltering an outdoor living room. In addition to housing common functions like cooking, laundry, and exercise facilities, the entire main floor is devoted to open-air living. On two sides, a grid of screens takes the place of solid walls. Other windows dissolve on command. The dining room's huge glass planes open via a pulley system devised by frequent collaborator Turner Exhibits, renowned for fabricating inventive kinetic elements: as the glass slides down a track and drops out of sight, a counterweighted handrail rises up. (They only want the effect of a death-defying overlook, not the real thing.) Reclining in a wicker armchair at sunset, in the company of a warm summer breeze, you'd think you were on a covered porch. "We like to confuse the barrier between the natural and the manmade," says Wise.

A short walk away, the two-story cabin where guests actually stay is distinguished by a similarly porous boundary. Each of the three bedrooms has its own sleeping porch should one prefer a plein air snooze. Indeed, almost every room throughout the property annexes an adjacent covered space, which not only doubles the square footage during warmer months but also intensifies the relationship with the lake. Interiors by Mimi London reinforce that connection; she chose finishes and fabrics in sage and ochre to mimic the surrounding greenery. "Half the time guests don't know if they are inside or outside—you really are fooled," London explains. "There is more to the property than just the lake; this lets you feel the architecture in its entire context."

Stone Creek Camp's centerpiece is the main house, whose facade is crafted from what appears to be stacked firewood. "This was our rebellious answer to our clients' request for a traditional log cabin," says Wise. A zigzagging staircase of bent steel ascends from a boulder-strewn garden to a green roof, which—when seen from above—makes the building dissolve into the hillside. With its elemental geometry, expressive surfaces, and lack of overt references to traditional residential architectural forms (nearly invisible windows, a hidden entryway), the design has the effect of an earthwork—a monumental sculpture in the tradition of Robert Smithson or Walter De Maria. "We thought of it as a piece of environmental art," notes Andersson.

Inside, the palette is almost disarmingly simple: vertical-grain Douglas fir ceilings, plate steel countertops, painted cabinetry, fireplaces of stacked stone. The rooms themselves prove surprisingly intimate for what appears, from the outside, to be quite a monumental space; the living room ceiling is just eight feet high. "We had Rudolph Schindler's own house in mind," says Andersson. "It feels quite cave-like and sheltering." He credits this largely to the juxtaposition of London's French-inflected industrial-chic décor against the rough-hewn architectural backdrop. Sleek steel tables and quirky '30s light fixtures intermingle with Adirondack chairs and custom wicker pieces inspired by old lodge furniture. "Arthur and Chris's use of material and scale is so powerful," says London. "I wanted to make sure that the spaces felt approachable and not overwhelming."

As with most of Andersson-Wise's projects, the design and placement of windows greatly inform the spatial experience. Where perpendicular log walls intersect, they pull apart to make room for full-height planes of glass, which seem to offer a portal to the elements, rather than a buffer from them. A frameless floor-to-ceiling window beside the living room fireplace appears open to the outdoors. A steel window cut into the adjacent wall was designed to store cordwood; removing a log invites the impression that you are pulling it right out of the facade. Above, a small spirit window deeper than it is tall grabs flashes of eastern light.

Opposite is a row of eight-foot-high sliding glass walls opening to a covered terrace curtained in white hemp. The drapes can be drawn shut against the sunset glare, further blurring the line between indoors and out. "Summer days here are long; you get a powerful blast of sun to the south between 6 and 10 PM," says London. "But the light is so riveting in this part

of Montana that you want to enjoy it any way you can." For this reason, the sliding panels are left open in the winter, too. "The clients just light a fire and wrap up in a bearskin," says Andersson. "That, to me, is what prospect and refuge is all about: communing with nature then retreating back into a room that's still engaged with the view, but elevated above the ground so you feel safe."

The partners relish the exquisite tensions between the grand and the intimate, the monumental and the personal. This quality, says London, is a byproduct of Andersson-Wise's exactitude. "When I joined the project, Arthur handed me about thirty pounds of blueprints—their work is that thorough and refined," she continues. "Their spaces may appear to be simple, but they are surprisingly complex." She pauses. "I think the design has to be that complicated and controlled to feel that simple and powerful." Although rooms segue into one another seamlessly to invite the impression of continuity and flow, subtle changes in ceiling height and proportion, for instance, conspire to make each space feel quite different when you are in them.

That spatial complexity is the legacy of Charles Moore, who mentored both partners.

Moore's artistic exuberance is best understood by visiting his expressionistic Austin home. The property, including part of a courtyard complex that once housed living quarters and the firm's original studio, is now owned by Moore's foundation. Everything in Moore's house is exactly as the fantasist left it, the product of an unbridled imagination. Walls are painted in overbold hues. Every surface is covered in curios. Panels of speckled tin line numerous walls. The kitchen is "carved" entirely from faux-marble plastic laminate. "He had an unparalleled sense of theater," notes Wise.

It was while working together on projects with Moore in Austin that Andersson and Wise discovered their shared values and creative compatibility. Since founding their firm, they have built a body of work that is uniquely their own—one that honors Moore's legacy by synthesizing his humanism and intelligence with a strong sense of structural and environmental integrity.

Their breakout project, completed in 2002, was the Chihuly Bridge of Glass in downtown Tacoma. The 470-foot-long pedestrian thoroughfare spans a freeway and rail lines to link the Museum of Glass with the Washington State History Museum, which Andersson and Moore designed in 1996. The bridge showcases glass artist Dale Chihuly's fantastical artworks within a series of pavilions. One suspends clusters of his colorful creations above a glass ceiling; passing through is like swimming underwater with a rainbow of sea creatures. A second pavilion is walled-in by display vitrines arrayed in a grid—a feature the partners repeated in Stone Creek Camp's screen windows and the Austin Lake House's trelliswork, where the larger structural grid of the building is replicated in miniature. The vitrines are encased in glass, so visitors simultaneously look *into* them to see the artworks and *through* them to survey the surrounding cityscape. The project was both well received and widely published, bringing a new kind of attention to the practice. It also established what has since become Andersson-Wise's trademark: designs that are by turns fragile and tough, immaterial and rock solid.

One example of that duality is the Duval County home of Buddy and Ellen Temple, on the southern tip of Texas. This is ranch country: prize deer, quarter horses, and Tennessee Walkers roam the sprawling 11,000-acre property, dotted with mesquite and oak trees that sprout from blossoming meadows. Ellen, who sits on the board of the Lady Bird Johnson Wildflower Center, has been slowly restoring the prairie's natural vegetation (and its butterfly population) since the couple purchased the site fifteen years ago; stewardship of the land was thus central to the architectural program. "The goal was to build something tethered to the site," Andersson explains.

Built from earthen bricks, a trio of low-slung houses quotes the deceptively elemental buildings of Bay Area modernist William Wurster, a major influence on Charles Moore—and, by extension, Andersson and Wise. That unassuming quality made sense here. "You don't make moves just to make them down here," Andersson explains. "The design is very pragmatic." Adds Wise: "The materials are all rough-hewn and textured, epitomized by the wood-mold bricks handmade just across the border in Mexico."

The natural beauty here, Andersson notes, is subtle rather than dramatic. "What's dramatic is the sense of openness." And, of course, the climate: "It's hotter there than you can imagine, even with prevailing winds from the southeast." Accordingly, the design is all about shelter and shade. Deep roof overhangs create comfortable porches; 110-degree afternoons are bearable thanks to breezes cooled by the concrete-edged pools beyond. Clerestories tucked below the tin roofs offer peek-a-boo views while screening direct light. In the main house—called the cottage—poured-concrete floors and plaster-skimmed walls feel cool to the touch and soften

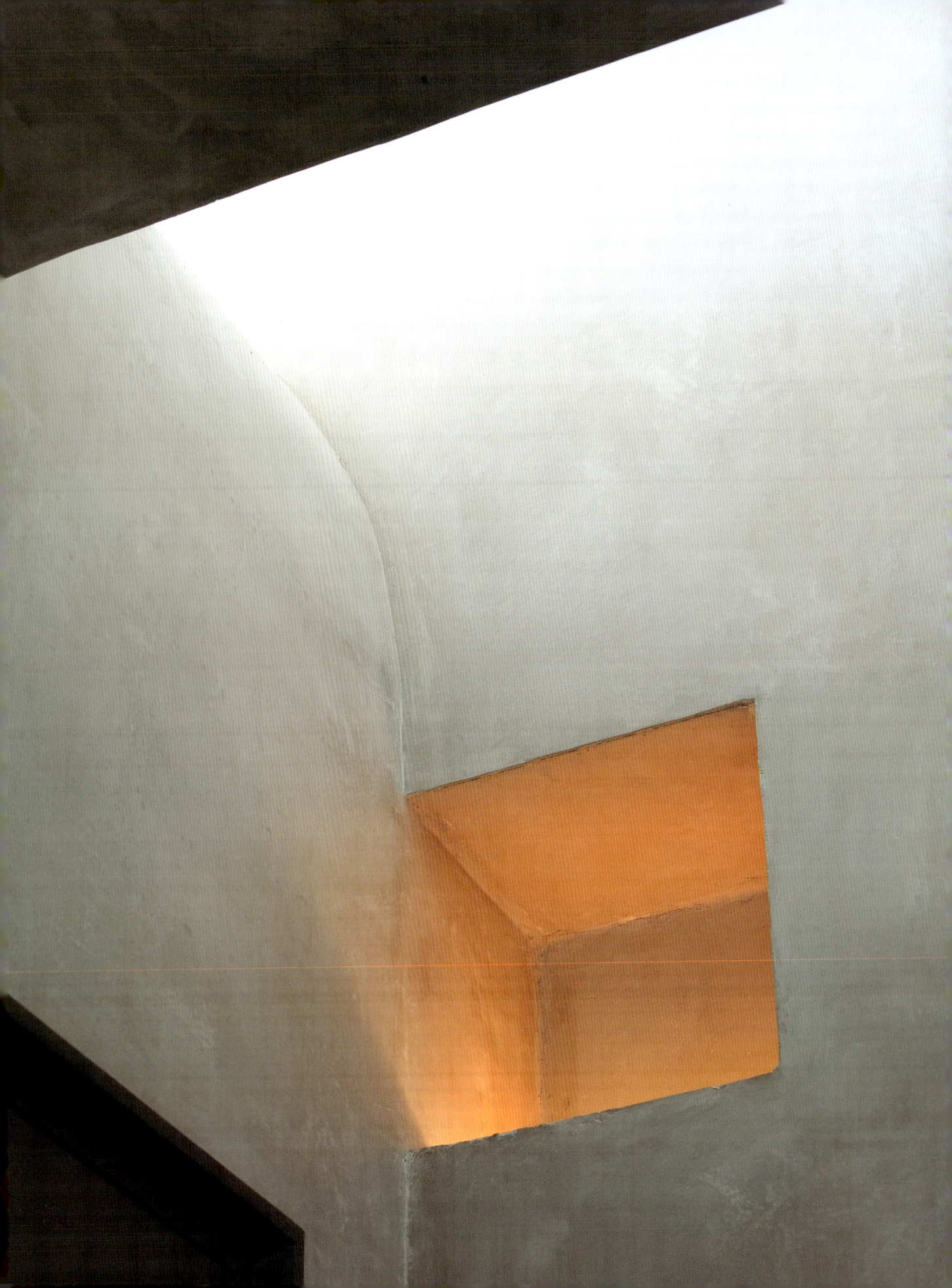

the bright sun. "The architecture is defensive by design: fortresslike, with thick walls punctured by tiny windows framing very specific vistas," says Andersson.

Fortresslike as they may seem when viewed from the vantage of the hot tub, inside the structures have an unexpected sense of openness. They are like two houses in one: a glass box, enveloped in floor-to-ceiling windows, that's been nested within a shell of brick and straight-grain pine. Mediating the two is a moat of space negotiating indoors and out: covered patios, light wells, screened-in porches. The architecture is both open and closed, sleek and textured, exhibitionist at the core—yet outwardly self-effacing.

Unlike many firms with multiple principles, both Andersson and Wise contribute to every project. Their collaboration is a pas de deux that marries fine art and exquisite craftsmanship. "The initial ideation is a back-and-forth," says Andersson. "But then I take the lead on composing the form and Chris burrows down and makes sure that what we do is craft. When we're working together, we are each in our element, firing on all cylinders." While each partner has his area of expertise, both are equally engaged in concept and execution, composition and detailing, and toggle back and forth seamlessly between scales.

The partners evolve designs by hand, eschewing computer renderings in favor of paper and pen. Andersson uses watercolor to capture the vibe of the project as well as its massing and volume. The medium, with its washy brushstrokes, lets him tease out the atmospheric quality he wants to achieve. "The act of painting forces me to figure out the light in a way that two-dimensional drawings just can't," he explains. "Elevations and sections come only after we've designed three dimensionally—they are not the means to organize our ideas." Wise then uses the watercolors to guide his own elaborate drawings. This marriage of big picture and small scale results in incredibly resolved spaces. No matter where your eye lands—a hinge, the joint between two materials—you notice superbly considered detailing.

Obsessing about minutiae doesn't end at the drawing board. Much is refined and finessed on-site. Take Stone Creek's stacked-firewood walls. "Once we decided to use logs in cross section, we had to figure out how it could function as an insulating wall," Wise recalls. He collaborated with the contractor to make four-by-four-foot mockups testing various stacking and bonding methods. "Originally we were going to use chinking—the goo that holds logs in place in traditional log-cabin construction—to act as the moisture barrier," he explains. "But it took up too much visual space." Thus the decision was made to split the logs and make a tighter fit with fewer gaps between. In the final design, logs are stacked on either side of an insulated structural wall whose exterior is sheathed in a waterproofing membrane. Each log is individually fitted and mechanically fastened to the wall, made of steel columns supporting a steel box frame. This configuration preserves the effect of stacked logs, while resulting in a weather-tight interior.

Solutions like this speak volumes about Andersson-Wise's thoughtful approach. Tellingly, both partners find greater inspiration in art and literature than in the canon of architectural history or the polyglot stew of contemporary culture. Conversations with Andersson-Wise about their work bring forth references to agony in J. M. W. Turner's watercolors, descriptive language in Italo Cavino's *Invisible Cities*, Roderick Nash's essays on depictions of landscape in American art, or the sense of light in seventeenth century Dutch paintings. Michelangelo's unfinished marble sculptures, for instance, inspired the House above Lake Austin, built on a high, rocky bluff overlooking the water. The low structure has chunky masonry walls skimmed with light-catching plaster; the effect is of a clean-lined volume being pushed out of a wild landscape. "Many sculptors carve out an overall shape and then continually refine it; Michelangelo, in contrast, would carve a perfect arm out of a rough block of marble—and then move onto the next body part," says Andersson. "That is what Chris and I aspired to here: this smooth stucco building that appears to be chiseled directly out of the rock." A highbrow reference? Sure. But not highfalutin. "The power of art is not appreciated solely on an intellectual level," he continues. "You can only take it in if you're emotionally invested."

Emotional investment is the key to understanding Andersson-Wise's architecture. Their work mainlines into your senses. You feel these spaces. They are wonderful to be in, full of light and atmosphere. They are not theoretical exercises; indeed, the only message their buildings seem to offer is: Design can be this good! For this reason, the partners blanch at the term *postmodernists* even while they grudgingly embrace it. "We do have a concern for spatial complexity and light play that is rooted in premodernist traditions," says Wise. "But postmodernism is such a loaded topic in architecture and, like all movements, presumes a certain ideological agenda. I dislike when architects talk about what their work means or the ideas it may manifest. We've always resisted that; ideology doesn't move us."

This puts them at odds with today's culture of chest-beating starchitects more concerned with Big Ideas than with making spaces people want to hang out in. Within this context, Andersson-Wise has a radical agenda indeed: imbuing day-to-day activities with poetry and awe. They are proposing a new way of living that's more in tune with the environment—and your psyche. Their designs address pragmatic needs but also a psychological yearning for refuge and contemplation, centering and escape, joy and comfort. And mental breathing room: "Good architecture leaves plenty of room for the mind to wander," says Andersson. "It's why I love ruins. I think it was Ruskin who said that the unfinished quality of ruins creates a blank space for you to complete with your imagination." Andersson grew up exploring the San Fernando Valley's half-built missions and the remains of old adobe houses. Later, while studying architecture in London, he spent weekends visiting the crumbling castles of rural England. "I loved how materially evident they are—there was so much mass and density to them." Appreciation for these remnants of the past even inspired Andersson-Wise's design of Temple Ranch: the main house is sited so that the living spaces overlook the skeletal foundation of the property's original 1850s structure, built from sillar stone—a kind of local masonry that bears the falling-apart look of early Roman buildings.

Andersson sees ruins not as a symbol of destruction, but as proof of how well architecture can resist the ravages of Father Time, when painstakingly crafted in regionally appropriate, aesthetically timeless materials—a lesson they apply to their own practice. These homes are heirloom pieces, meant to be passed from generation to generation. They linger not just on the earth but also in your memory—leaving an impression long after you've walked away.

House Above Lake Austin

Austin, Texas, 2002

Spanish Colonial Revival buildings trace their origins from the hot climates of Moorish Spain and North Africa to Mexico and California. They are characterized by masonry and stucco walls, which absorb heat and reflect light to create cool, dark, quiet refuges from the sun.

This house above Lake Austin represents a modern transformation of the environmentally responsive Spanish style. Sited on a cliff, with terraces that descend a steep hill, the building's simple materials celebrate the site and climate not by drawing attention to them, but by blending in. The stone foundation of this house similarly is tied to the natural stone of the mountain. Smooth plaster walls above the foundation appear to have been chiseled from the rock itself. Out of the rough-hewn rock above the river comes a sculpted domicile. The exterior walls are gray, burnished stucco, and interior walls are a creamy, natural plaster. But the initial appearance of simplicity is misleading.

A sheltered entry, one of the few visible apertures on the front facade of the building, leads into a foyer flanked by the living room and dining room. High, small windows illuminate the interior of the building, but are configured so the sun only rarely shines directly into them. During the course of the day, natural light defines how the house is used. Morning light illuminates the kitchen and breakfast area and transforms the living room into a soft, golden hue in the evening. Deep recesses within the exterior walls allow rooms to be sunny in the winter and shaded in the summer. The plan configuration is subtly shifted and the ceiling plane shaped to allow light to bend and trace deep into the interior spaces of the house. The result is light that changes constantly as it plays on the plaster walls that define each space. One is drawn from room to room by illuminated surfaces punctuated with deep shadows. Similarly, from the exterior, deeply recessed openings contrast with large wall surfaces brightly illuminated by the sun.

Floor to ceiling sliding wooden doors add to the drama and allow the owners to regulate air-conditioned space, room by room. The size of the house, therefore, is easily transformed, depending on how many people are using it. This is a boon in the summer months, when every effort to improve the efficiency of cooling systems is necessary.

View of lower terrace and north facade of master suite

overleaf:
View of entrance from garden

Entrance

(counterclockwise from top):
Entry from driveway
Window detail
Entrance detail

(counterclockwise from top):
Living room
Living room alcove
View to dining room

opposite:
View through stone window from living room

Dormer at dusk

opposite:
Butler's pantry lit by dormer

View of north facade

(counterclockwise from top):
Detail of stone window
Stone window
Stairs to terrace

overleaf:
View looking south at dusk

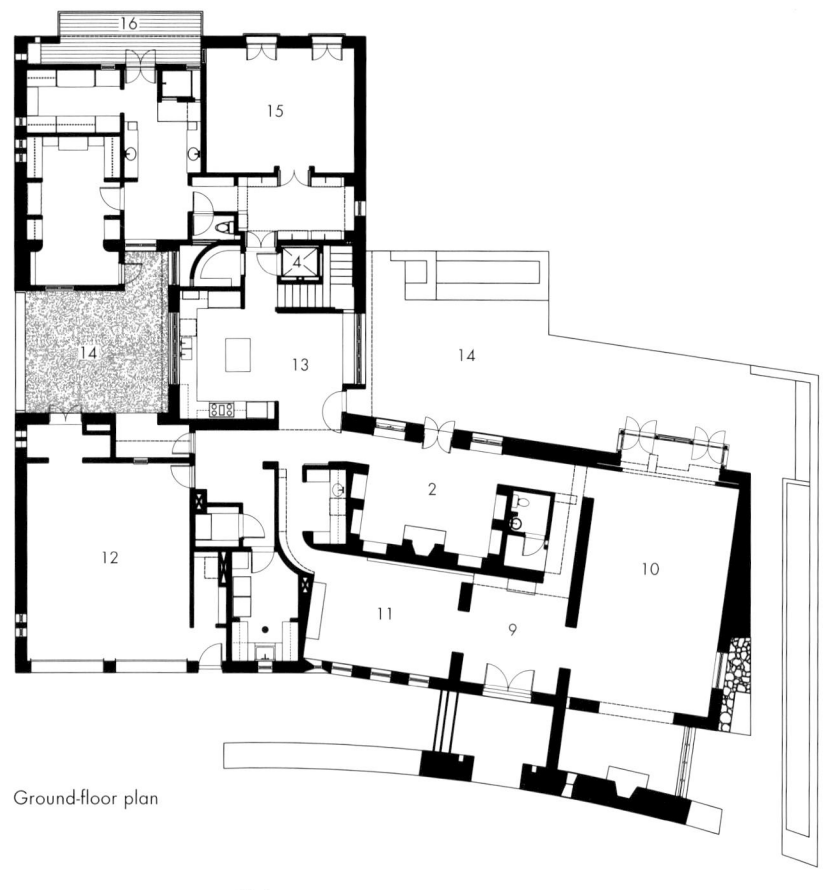

Ground-floor plan

1 Bedroom
2 Family room
3 Future bedroom
4 Elevator
5 Storage
6 Sewing room
7 Utility
8 Bathroom
9 Foyer
10 Living room
11 Dining room
12 Garage
13 Kitchen
14 Terrace
15 Master bedroom
16 Balcony

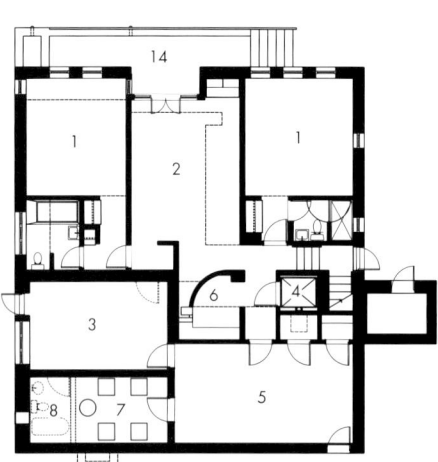

House Above Lake Austin lower-floor plan

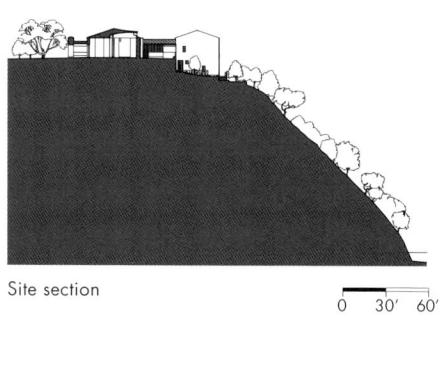

Site section

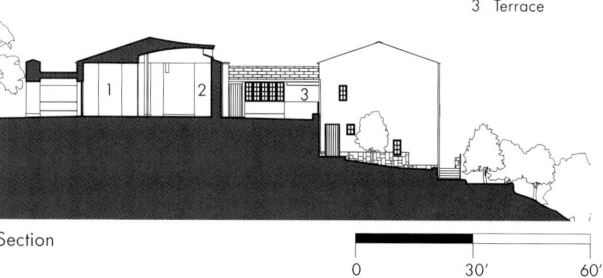

Section

1 Entry
2 Powder Room
3 Terrace

72  Natural Houses

(counterclockwise from top):
View of north facade at dusk
West facade
View to lake from lower terrace

(counterclockwise from top):
View looking north from terrace
View looking north from second-floor balcony
View of lake from terrace

opposite:
View of stairs from lower terrace

Stone Creek Camp
Bigfork, Montana, 2008

This remote Montana compound is entered gradually by descending a narrow gravel road through the deep vegetation of a northern primordial forest. About a mile into the pilgrimage, the forest opens to a dramatic expanse of land, sky, and water. Flathead Lake reaches into the distance. A pair of stark, substantive gatehouses greets the visitor, while the arrangement of buildings in the camp below embodies the notion of prospect and refuge as put forth by the English geographer Jay Appleton in his book *The Experience of Landscape*. It is the unexpected opportunity to see combined with the ability to hide in a protected space that reinforces aesthetic satisfaction. Being here, one can experience the lake, with its view, grandeur, and promise. At the same time, the rooms of these structures provide an intimate sense of being in a protected place.

    The Camp is situated along a sloping hill, leading visitors to discover the site progressively. From the gatehouses, a pebble and earth path leads down the hill to the Master House, the Main Lodge, and the Guesthouse. The buildings offer warm, almost cavelike spaces as well as expansive porches, open to the sunlight and views. They are designed to let people feel the natural environment, indoors and outdoors. Small windows and thick walls facing into the slope of the site are contrasted with entire walls that open up toward the lake. The two-foot-thick cordwood wall on the upper side of the Master House is constructed with a double wythe of wood and an insulated waterproof layer in the middle. The cordwood is dry stacked and attached to the center insulated wall using blind fasteners. The result is a commodious structure connected materially with the site. Inhabitants may choose to be outdoors while inside by sliding open the walls and moving outside to spaces that are more civilized than the outlying wilderness. Similarly, with each bedroom's separate, screened-in space, it is always possible to sleep in nature and yet still be secure within the building.

    The materials and textures of the buildings connect them to the site. Like the lake, they feel as if they have been—and will be—here forever. The effect is paradoxical: despite their size, the camp's large structures seem to emerge from the rock, wood, and grasses that surround them.

View from above Master House looking west toward Flathead Lake

Master House (counterclockwise from top):
Entry courtyard at dusk
Entry courtyard looking northwest
North facade of courtyard

Stone and cordwood wall detail

overleaf:
Master House, entry courtyard

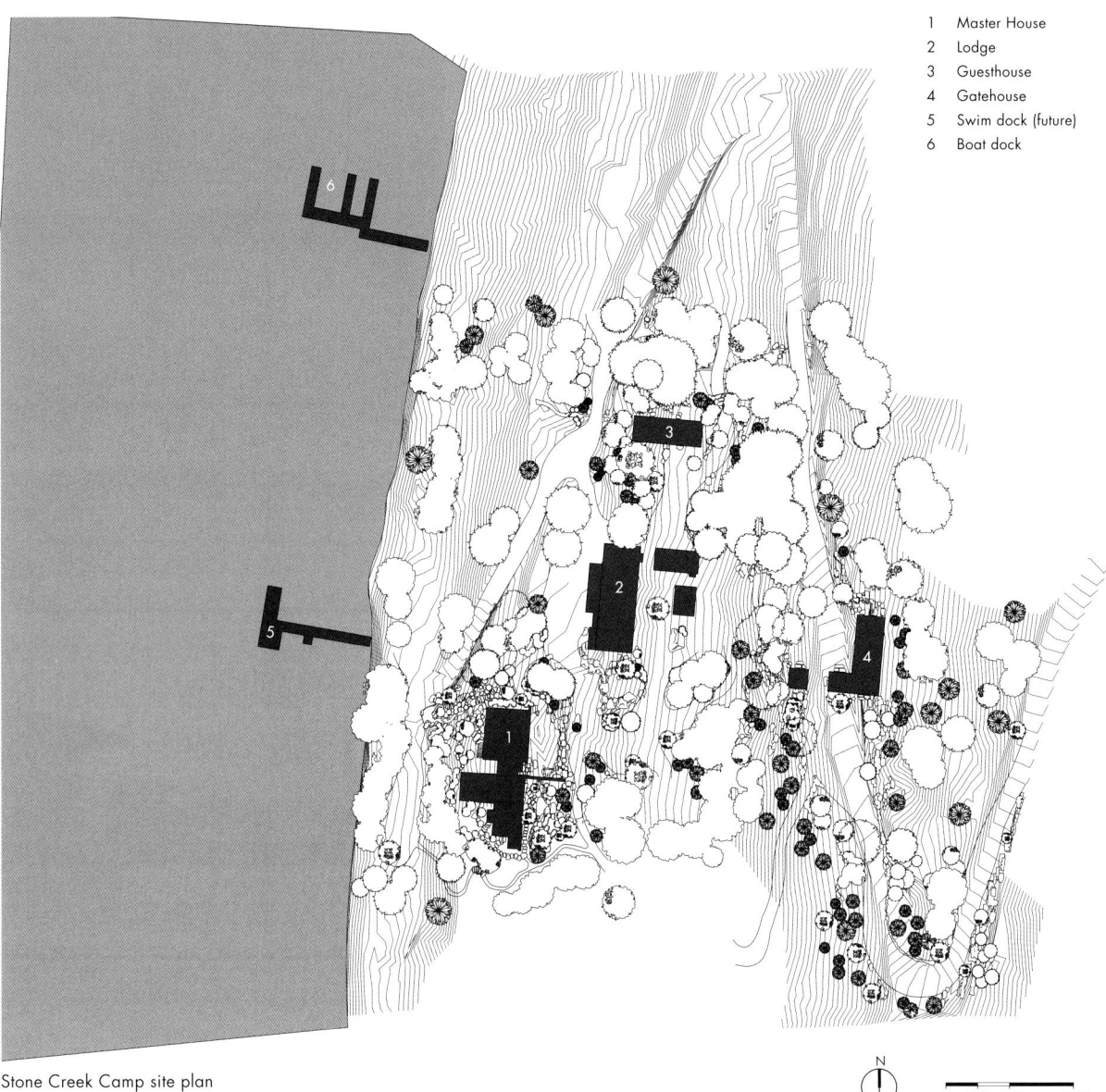

Stone Creek Camp site plan

1 Master House
2 Lodge
3 Guesthouse
4 Gatehouse
5 Swim dock (future)
6 Boat dock

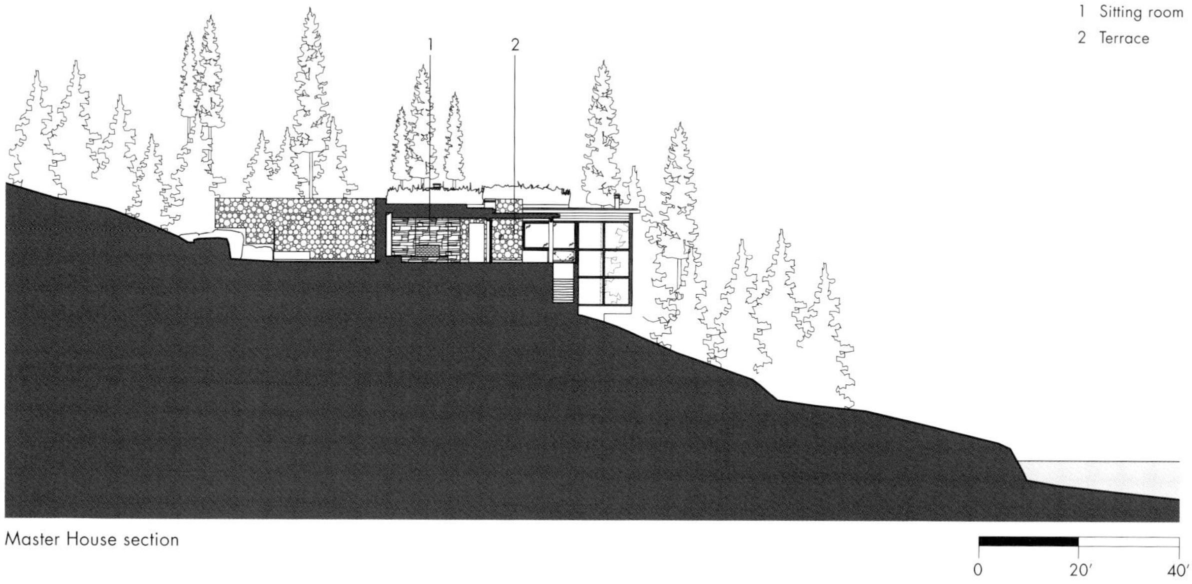

1 Sitting room
2 Terrace

Master House section

1 Entry
2 Sitting room
3 Kitchen
4 Office
5 Terrace
6 Master bedroom
7 Sleeping porch
8 Master bathroom
9 Master closet
10 Outdoor shower

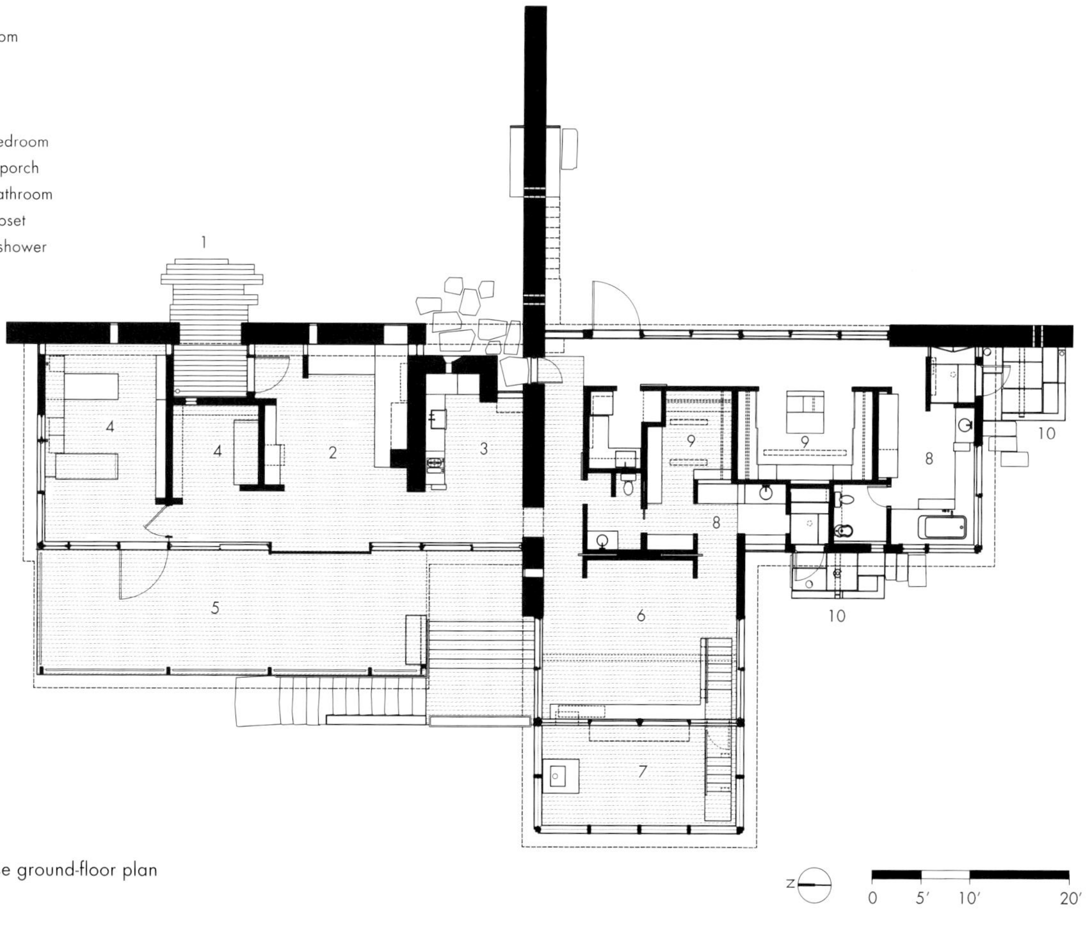

Master House ground-floor plan

83   Stone Creek Camp

Master House (top to bottom):
Sitting room
Kitchen

opposite:
Kitchen detail

Master House outdoor shower

opposite:
View of Master House roof from south

overleaf:
Master House west facade

Master House, view of lake from terrace

Master House (top to bottom):
Terrace
Terrace looking north

Master House, sleeping porch looking north

opposite:
Sleeping porch looking south

(clockwise from top):
Approach to Gatehouse
Gatehouse roof detail
Steel sign at private drive

overleaf:
Guesthouse second-floor sleeping
  porch looking south

1. Exercise room
2. Bathroom
3. Outdoor living room
4. Living room
5. Mud room

Lodge section

1. Sleeping porch
2. Bedroom
3. Kitchen
4. Outdoor sitting room

Guesthouse section

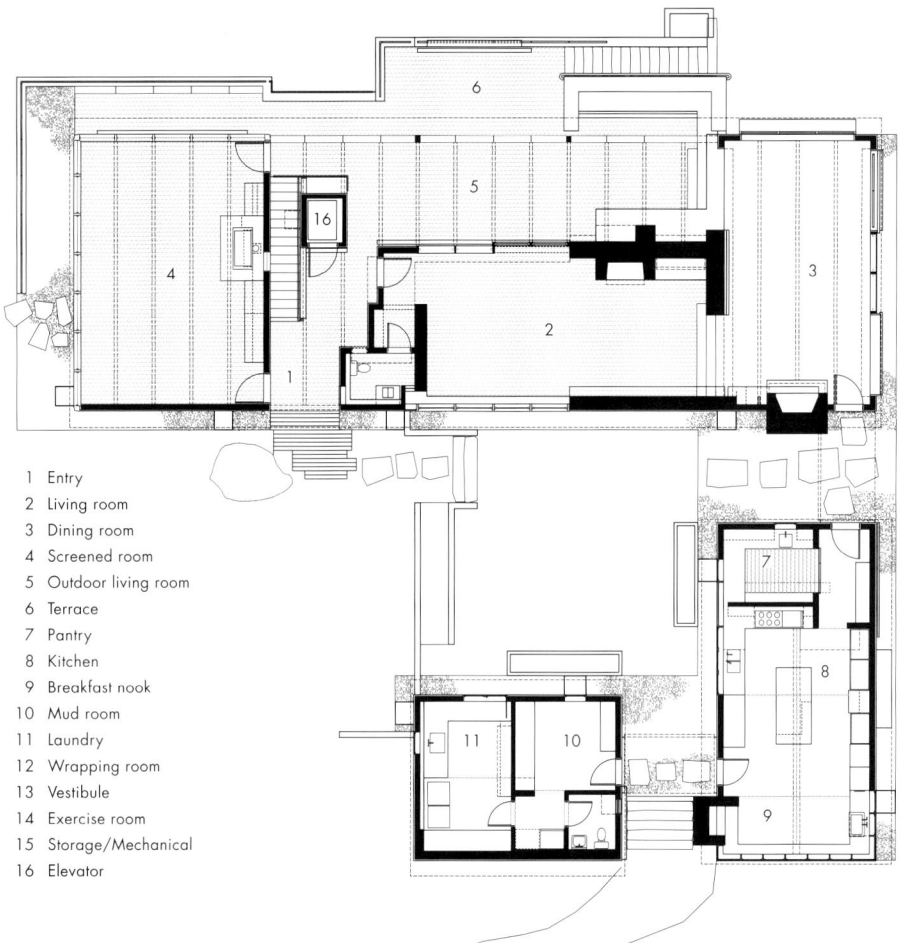

1 Entry
2 Living room
3 Dining room
4 Screened room
5 Outdoor living room
6 Terrace
7 Pantry
8 Kitchen
9 Breakfast nook
10 Mud room
11 Laundry
12 Wrapping room
13 Vestibule
14 Exercise room
15 Storage/Mechanical
16 Elevator

Ground-floor plan

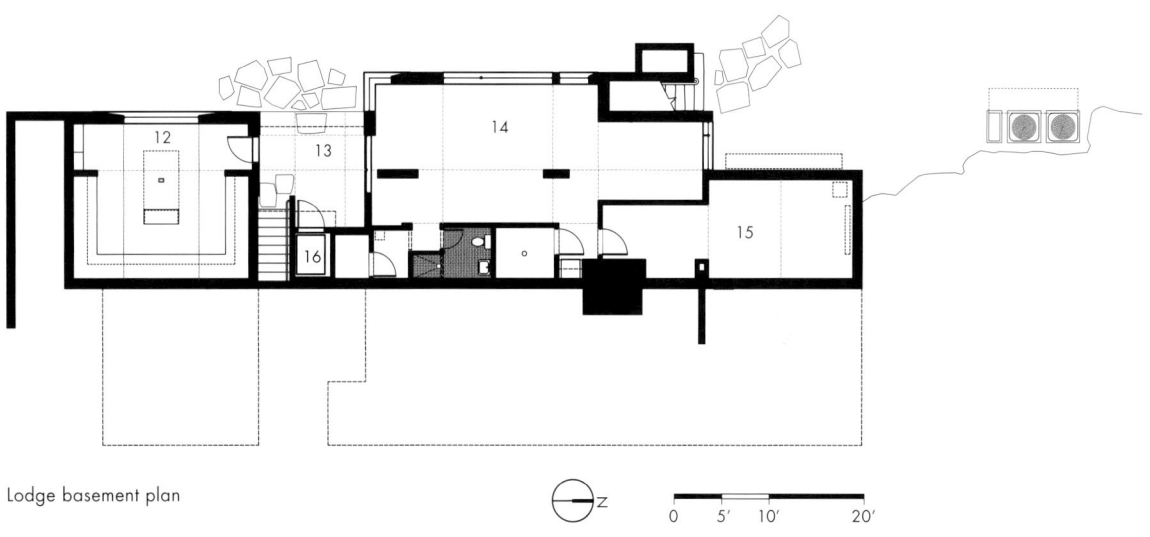

Lodge basement plan

Lodge (top to bottom):

Indoor outdoor dining room

Crank mechanism for moveable wall

Lodge, dining room window and balcony in closed position

Lodge, dining room window and balcony in open position

Guesthouse barn door detail

Guesthouse (clockwise from top):
View looking northwest
Outdoor shower
Southwest corner

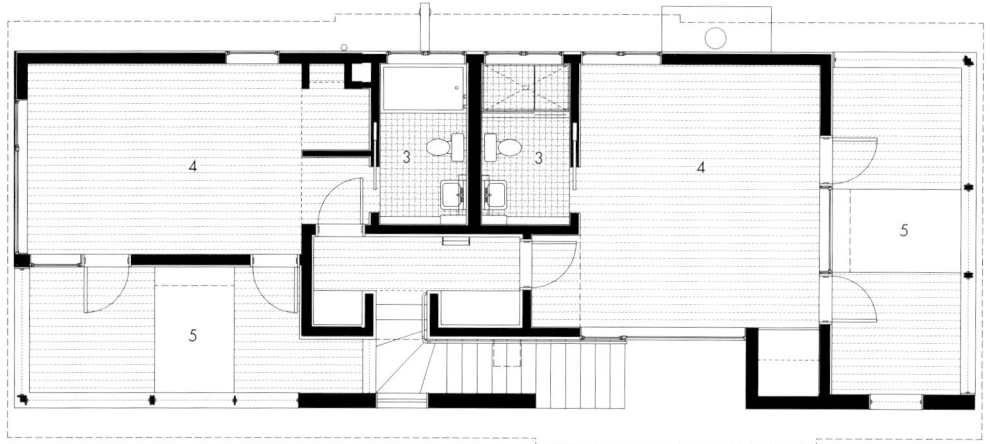

Second-floor plan

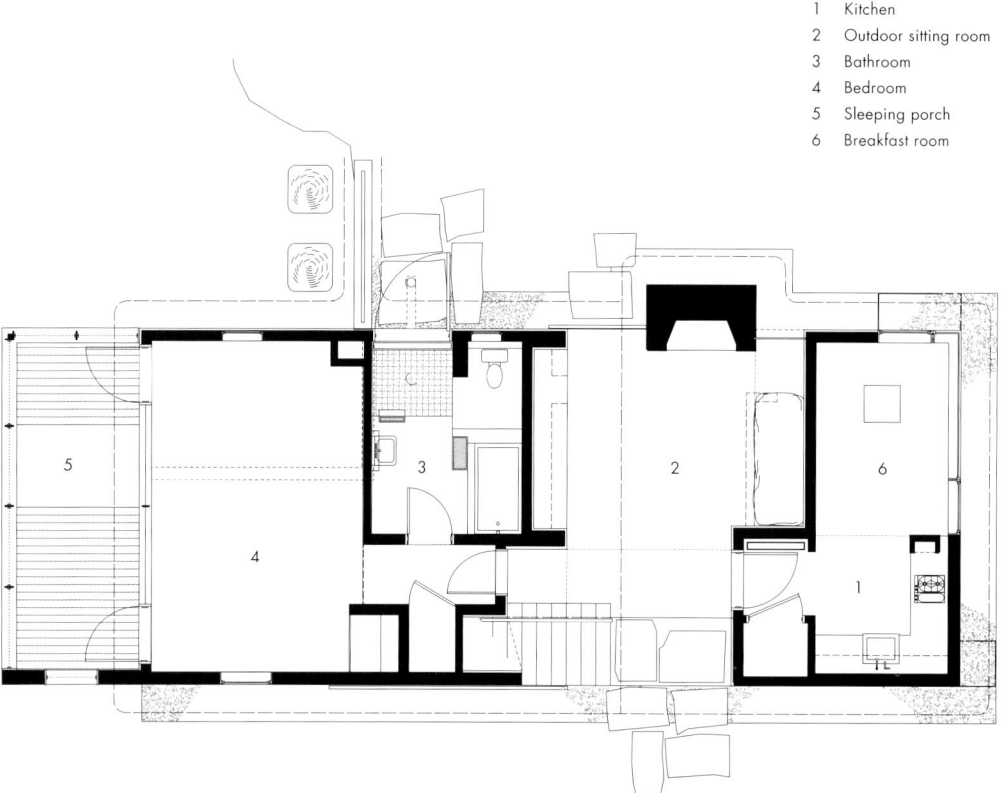

1 Kitchen
2 Outdoor sitting room
3 Bathroom
4 Bedroom
5 Sleeping porch
6 Breakfast room

Guesthouse ground-floor plan

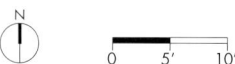

104  Natural Houses

Guesthouse (top to bottom):
Second-floor sleeping porch looking west
Outdoor sitting room

overleaf:
Boat dock on Flathead Lake

On the Salubrity of Sites:
The Residential Architecture of Arthur Andersson and Chris Wise
Frederick Steiner

The houses designed by Austin-based architects Arthur Andersson and Chris Wise accomplish twin apparently competing goals. Their buildings appear contemporary, evoking ideas and feelings about our current condition, while fitting seamlessly into the environments that they inhabit. The work appears as if it has always been there, imbuing its context with a sense of participation.

Fresh out of architecture school at the University of Kansas, Andersson met Charles Moore in the late summer of 1980. Moore later chose Andersson to be his and William Turnbull's assistant during the building of the Wonderwall at the 1984 Louisiana World Exposition. After Moore moved to Austin to become the first O'Neil Ford Chair at The University of Texas, he invited Andersson to manage his new office there.

Moore and Andersson envisioned a Texas Taliesin and bought a piece of property in the heart of Austin to realize that vision. They set up a makeshift office in Moore's living room and added a design studio, transforming the house into a compound. The studio was established around a dedicated group of architects that included Chris Wise, who had earned a degree from the University of Texas at Austin in 1987. In this context, Andersson and Wise began their careers under the tutelage of a mentor who devoted much of his life to the design of houses.

Chris Wise worked with Moore/Andersson Architects until 1991, when he went to work for Donlyn Lyndon, one of Moore's original partners at MLTW, in Berkeley, California. He later received a Master of Design Studies from Harvard in 1995 and then returned to Austin to work with Andersson. Even after Moore passed away in 1993, the firm remained Moore/Andersson until 2001, when Wise became a partner and the name was changed to Andersson-Wise Architects. Their work came to distinguish itself from that of Moore.

"We studied alternative strategies," Andersson declares, "and became drawn to materials of consequence, materials that look better, not worse, over time."

As a result of their interest in what it takes to be comfortable in a given climate, the material quality of the buildings is palpable. Their buildings are situated with careful consideration for how they will age. The fascination with how buildings can withstand time has drawn Andersson to look closely at ruins. "With ruins," he notes, "you can fill in the spaces left blank by time."

Following Moore's death, much of the firm's work focused on residential projects. Their houses, like ruins, provide a canvas where the residents fill in the open spaces. A residence in the foothills of the Catalina Mountains near Tucson, Arizona, designed in Moore/Andersson's last years, stands out in its response to climate and context. Connie and Martin Stone's home, completed in 1995, minimizes energy consumption by using the opportunities and constraints of its harsh, yet beautiful, surroundings. An evaporative cooling system combined with massive adobe walls, and careful orientation to capture breezes within the desert climate. The house offers expansive views of the city of Tucson on one side and the Catalina Mountains on the other. The large openings that engage these views are in alignment with prevailing breezes. The architects took on energy and environmental concerns with this house before the recent rapid expansion of interest in green design and before the widespread application of sustainable design tools.

The Stones were so pleased with their desert home that they embarked on a new project with Andersson and Wise, this one on the sloping shores of Flathead Lake near Big Fork, Montana. If designing in the desert was about protection from harsh sunlight, designing this compound in northern Montana was an exercise in bringing sunlight into buildings and their surrounding spaces. The result is four buildings carefully sited on a series of terraces leading to a boat dock and a future swim dock. In addition to the main house, the complex includes a gatehouse, a guesthouse, and a lodge.

More than buildings, the structures in the Stone Crook Camp are modified porches, open to the warmth of the sun and views of Flathead Lake. With close consideration of terrain, the design displays masterful use of its site allowing the outdoors and the indoors to flow together seamlessly. When trees were cut, the wood was reused as a building material. For example, the master house includes stunning cordwood walls, evoking the giant firewood piles visible across the American West. These walls are powerful in their humility. The image is of something that is new, yet seems to have always been there.

Flathead Lake is a glacial moraine, and the building appears to be an outgrowth of the natural granite that inhabits the site. On the upslope side of the site, the more solid aspects of the building are made of rocks

and wood. The same rock wall that defines the entrance to the master house extends to the roof through the fireplace chimney, nestled among native stem grass. The rigorously resolved detailing of the stone walls combines with a precise, wood framework to reveal a completely modern building made from a traditional palette.

The grass roof of the master house is an example of the intelligent plant use. During the summer the roof is green, blending into the forest so that from the vantage point of the lodge and other upslope buildings, it virtually disappears. During the autumn, the dry grass stands out like a shaggy head of bright yellow hair. Andersson and Wise arranged the building on the site to allow the underground springs to flow naturally to the lake. Native vegetation helps to direct water flow and absorb stormwater as these hearty plants have controlled water flow to the lake for centuries.

The buildings are arranged to capture sunlight and to reduce energy use. In their Tuson House, the Andersson-Wise design minimized air conditioning with intelligent site planning and thick walls. In Montana, the buildings have no central heating, which Andersson calls "kinda crazy." Instead, fireplaces and radiant heating accomplish this goal. The overall site plan encourages the Stones to use the outdoors, but in protected, comfortable spaces.

Also on Flathead Lake, Andersson-Wise designed a cabin for Austin friends Lillian and Walter Loewenbaum. The cabin is sited on a rock outcropping on the slope below a cliff, where the ruins of old trees are home to families of ospreys. Six hand-cast concrete piers support the structure, hovering above the ground on stilts, and nested in the tall ponderosa pines and Douglas firs.

Only a screen protects visitors from the elements outside this delicately placed, handmade cabin. The structure is there for the sheer enjoyment of viewing the avian habitat and the dramatic environment of the tall trees and lake. The open-air, primitive hut is a return to the elements. Inside, Douglas fir, common in western Montana creates a warm, rustic environment. The cabin's indigenous materials and delicate placement make it feel like it belongs to the forest and the lake, with the osprey and the eagles, the elk and the bear.

"I've always been interested in Henry David Thoreau and the philosophy of allowing a relationship with nature to define the principles in one's life," Andersson observes. "Economy was a huge part of how

Thoreau lived. And it was economy, in form, impact, and materials, that drove the Loewenbaum cabin design. We conceived a simple palette of wood, detailed to enable the structure to be built by hand. Two people made this structure over a period of eight months."

In 2002, when the American Institute of Architects, Austin Chapter, design jury reviewed noteworthy projects, the Lake House on Lake Austin, designed by Andersson-Wise stood out for its beauty and simplicity. The images, including one of an exuberant boy leaping from the boathouse into the lake, were mesmerizing. "The simplicity of this project makes it one of the most satisfying we've built," explains Andersson. The 400-square-foot boathouse was made with three materials: ipe wood, steel, and screen. It is an open pavilion that encourages welcome breezes from the lake. Within the structural grid, operable panels invite a plunge into the cool waters below.

It is a pilgrimage to get there, but a 250-foot-long suspension bridge spanning a rocky gorge facilitates the journey. To keep the terrain undisturbed, footings were poured from a helicopter, which made fifteen separate trips to the site. The powerfully simple design of both elements claims the hillside and the lakeside with structures that miraculously exist within the rugged natural setting.

Traveling further west in Austin, one encounters a series of highland lakes that mark the transition to the Texas Hill Country. These lakes were developed in the 1930s as part of the Lower Colorado River Authority's water management program.

At Lake Travis, the largest of these lakes, a few of the early dwellings built of Texas limestone remain. Lynwood and Su Alice Jostes spent time at their lodge on the lake for many years and sought an addition to accommodate visits from their children, grandchildren, and friends. Instead of adding on, Andersson and Wise chose to construct a tower adjacent to the historically valuable structure. The location of the new building creates a courtyard nestled in the cedars and live oaks.

Within its 400-square-foot floor plan, the Tower House comprises three floors with a single bedroom and bath on each and an open air terrace at the top. Windows open to capture views and breezes from the lake. Walking up the stairs offers snapshots of the landscape as well as views—in, around, and through the building—before arriving at the rooftop terrace looking out to Lake Travis.

Expansive views are also a feature in a residence overlooking Lake Austin from Mount Bonnell, one of the tallest points in Central Austin. From this high spot, the views are spectacular, not only down the cliff to the lake, but across the Hill Country to the west. But from inside the house, the drama of the natural context is not presented in a conventional manner. Rather, carefully composed openings frame the panoramic scene. Several windows display the more intimate surroundings such as nearby walls and vegetation. A series of small terraces, built of locally quarried limestone, step down the slope, offering changing perspectives of the hills and water beyond.

These apertures, in walls and on the roof, grab light from the west in various ways so that natural light glows deep inside the house. Monolithic walls made of earth-colored plaster receive this glowing light. Shaped to accept and bend light, they create a highly sculptural architectural experience. As with the cordwood walls at the Stones's Flathead Lake house, the earthy plaster walls have a material presence that celebrates the characteristics of their place.

Walking around the house, which seems classical and contemporary at once, there is a remarkable feeling of connection to the natural landscape. Good site design involves learning how to read the landscape and then applying that literacy from the outside in. All of these residences certainly display masterful site design; however, the House Above Lake Austin best illustrates their skill at creating interior rooms that celebrate a connection to the landscape from within. The landscape can be read from within through captured light and view. One is compelled to move from inside to outside by virtue of the strength of these connections.

Over twenty centuries ago, the Roman architect Vitruvius emphasized the importance of site design in his classic treatise, *The Ten Books on Architecture*. According to Vitruvius, in a chapter devoted to the "salubrity of sites," the choice of a "very healthy site" was the first general principle to be observed. He wrote, "[I]f the building is on the coast with a southern or western exposure, it will not be healthy, because in summer the southern sky grows hot at sunrise and is fiery at noon, while a western exposure grows warm after sunrise, is hot at noon, and at evening all aglow."

Vitruvius urged us to design with nature in mind, setting the stage for what we now call sustainable design. The work of Andersson and Wise might be characterized as sustainable or green design. Within the School of Architecture at the University of Texas, we have ongoing debates about what constitutes sustainable design and whether it threatens creativity. Good design is sustainable, one argument goes. Labels can be dangerous, because they tend to pigeonhole architects into a style, be it modernism, postmodernism, or green architecture.

My view is that good design is indeed sustainable. Arthur Andersson and Chris Wise help bridge the supposed divide between sustainability and good design, by focusing on permanence and energy efficiency. They display creative and imaginative responses to specific places and programs.

Furthermore, we have no long-term choice but to build with restoration and regeneration in mind. The energy and resource demands of buildings are important considerations in a growing, urbanizing planet with finite resources. Austin, Texas, with its innovative Austin Energy Green Building program, provides an ideal base for architects to pursue designs that address these concerns.

Architecture is rooted in experiment and experience. Each Andersson-Wise project experiments with new forms, especially suited for a specific place. With every new residential project, the firm's experience in sustainable design—an architecture of permanence—has deepened and been enriched. Working with site-cast concrete, locally quarried stone, or indigenous wood, their experiments expand upon their sustainable roots with increasing boldness.

Andersson-Wise illustrates that high-quality distinctive design can be built to last. They have grown beyond their postmodern roots but continue to display a respect for place, context, and precedent. Their work neither shuns ornament nor adds superficial embellishment. Rather, their work captures the essence of a place, while contributing new meaning and understanding.

According to a Brookings Institution study conducted by Arthur Nelson, the United States is facing an unprecedented need for new buildings. Nelson projects that by 2030, half of the buildings where Americans live, work, and shop will have been built since 2000. We will clearly need to build more homes and build them in a more responsible, energy-efficient manner. Over the next twenty-five years, we will need architecture that connects us to our past and to our place, yet stimulates our senses. The work of Andersson-Wise guides the way toward an architecture that engages the natural world in a meaningful manner.

Collector's House
Austin, Texas, 2002

Set in the rolling hills of west Austin, the Collector's House is surrounded by a seductively private landscape full of gentle slopes and dense foliage. Its low-slung, wooden structure seems almost to recede into the shadows created by deep porches and tree shade. It was apparent as we spent some time inside that the sunlight from a series of overhead skylights was uncomfortably bright. This, combined with the fact that only a few windows allowed a connection to the trees outside, made an environment that was open and overly bright on the inside, yet closed to the outside. We worked to reverse this effect, softening the light from the sky by bending it around new surfaces at the ceiling level, and removing obstructions to the exterior views.

This renovation consisted of sculpting new space, focusing light on surfaces, and playing with its effects. The goal was to make the house into a gallery for the client's art collection and divide the rooms themselves into pictorial compositions. By creating protected spaces, where the light is brought in selectively, the rooms now impart a sense of calm and quiet. Every object is illuminated and infused with natural light, mysterious yet well defined. Within this minimal approach, niches, shelves, and alcoves exist to make carefully composed locations for artwork. The design focuses on surface color and texture. The palette consists of two materials: plaster and the neutral dark tone of the ebonized wood floor. Carefully placed windows and walls allow sunlight to define the shape and character of the rooms. Walls and ceilings adhere to a simple aesthetic. The new experience in this home is reminiscent of the works of Jan Vermeer, whose quiet paintings evoke a certain lifelike serenity.

Living room and stair to loft

Entry stair detail

(top to bottom):
View of pool and deck from east
View of spa pavilion from east

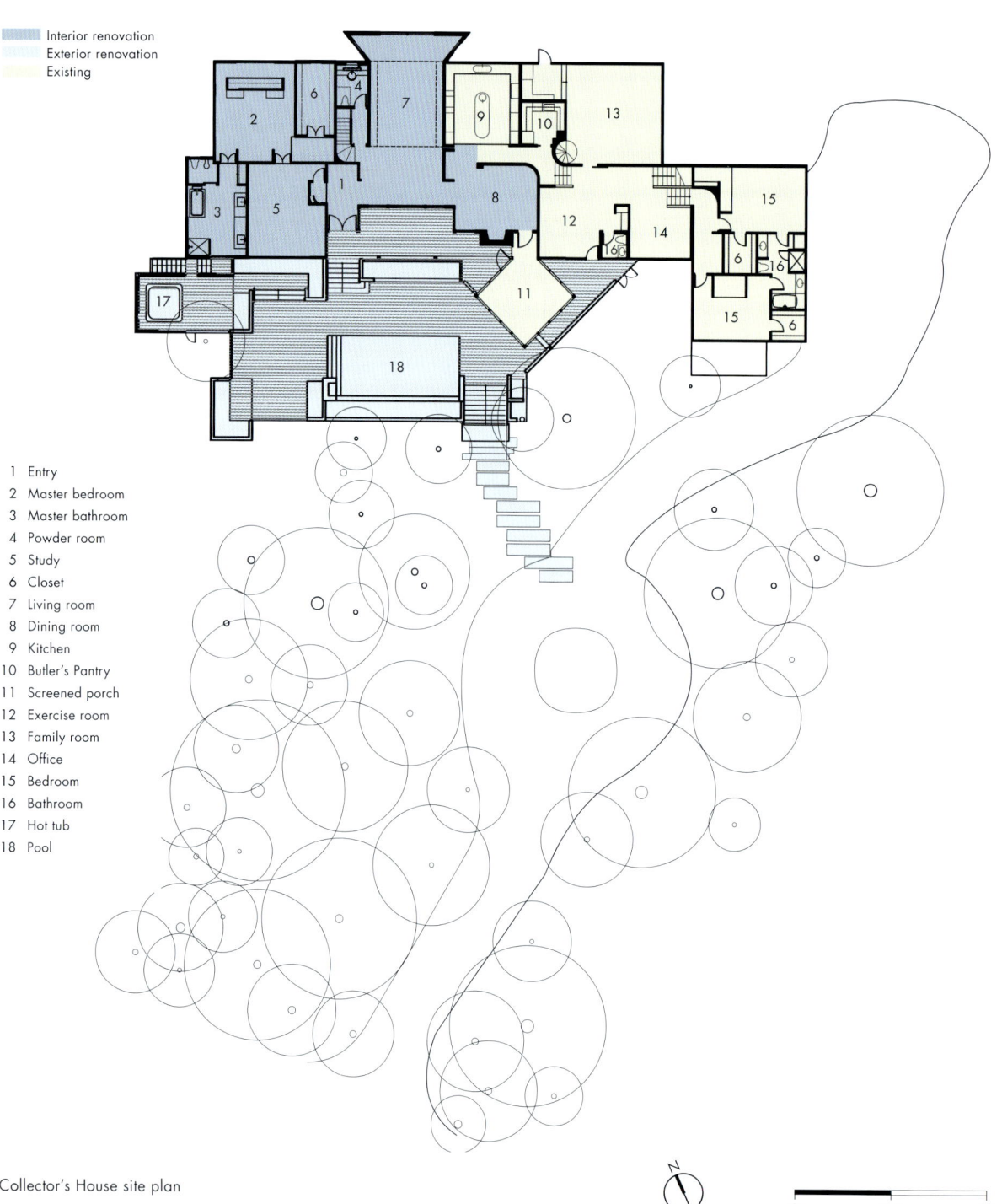

Interior renovation
Exterior renovation
Existing

1 Entry
2 Master bedroom
3 Master bathroom
4 Powder room
5 Study
6 Closet
7 Living room
8 Dining room
9 Kitchen
10 Butler's Pantry
11 Screened porch
12 Exercise room
13 Family room
14 Office
15 Bedroom
16 Bathroom
17 Hot tub
18 Pool

Collector's House site plan

Pool sitting area and fountain

overleaf:
View of pool from entry

Renovation
Existing

1 Guest loft
2 Bathroom
3 Mechanical room
4 Open to below

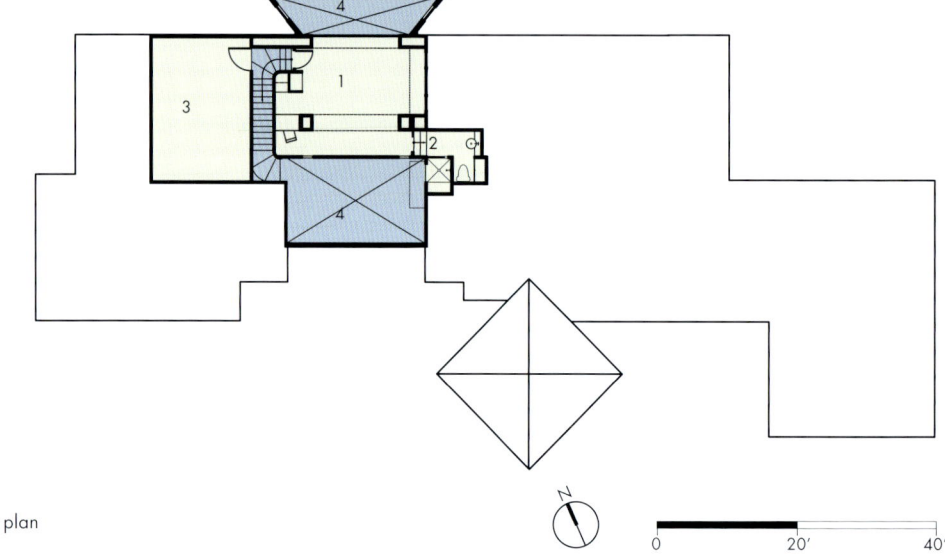

Collector's House upper-floor plan

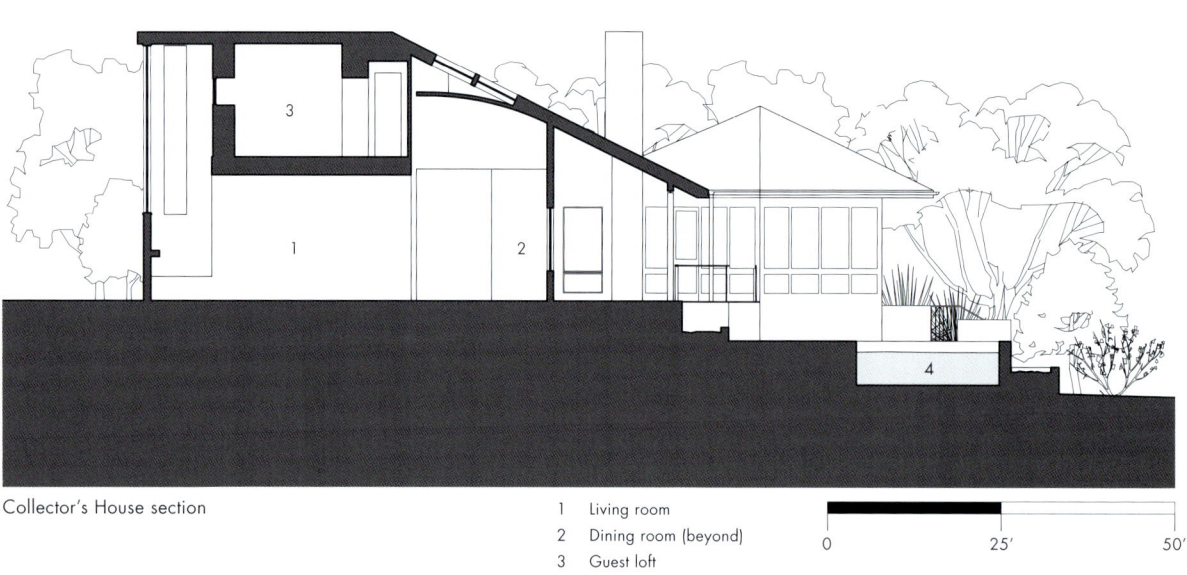

Collector's House section

1 Living room
2 Dining room (beyond)
3 Guest loft
4 Pool

(clockwise from top):
Entry terrace looking east
Entry terrace
Screen porch

(counterclockwise from top):
Tapestry detail
Living room
Living room detail

opposite:
Living room

overleaf:
Living room

(left to right):
Master bathroom
Powder room

Entry

Temple Ranch
Duval County, Texas, 2009

The primeval qualities of nature, the sun and wind, broad sky and rocky hard earth define the experience of South Texas. Everything that exists in this environment is essential. Trees, scrub, and wildflowers have evolved to subsist on little water, withstand a scorching brilliant sun and icy winds from the north. Life here must have a purpose in order to exist.

    As nature would have it, this environment is home to a bountiful population of native quail and deer that has been deemed some of the best in the southwest. Our project, known as the Temple Ranch, is the seasonal retreat for Buddy and Ellen Temple, who have for two decades passionately worked to manage, restore, and preserve the native habitat of this place. Their building program outlined the importance of making buildings that promote both social interaction and quiet contemplation. We considered the land and the gentle sloping terrain, the natural air-conditioning offered by prevailing breezes from the southeast, and the ever-present sun. Our observations transformed into an idea for structures that have a very tough outer shell of locally made brick. Deep open porches seem carved out of the exterior brick volumes, revealing transparent walls that slide open to the rooms inside. The buildings, a cottage, two guest houses, and the existing lodge, are organized around an open courtyard with a large swimming pool and spa, oriented to take advantage of the prevailing breezes.

Infinite edge pool and spa waterfall

overleaf:
View of Cottage looking south

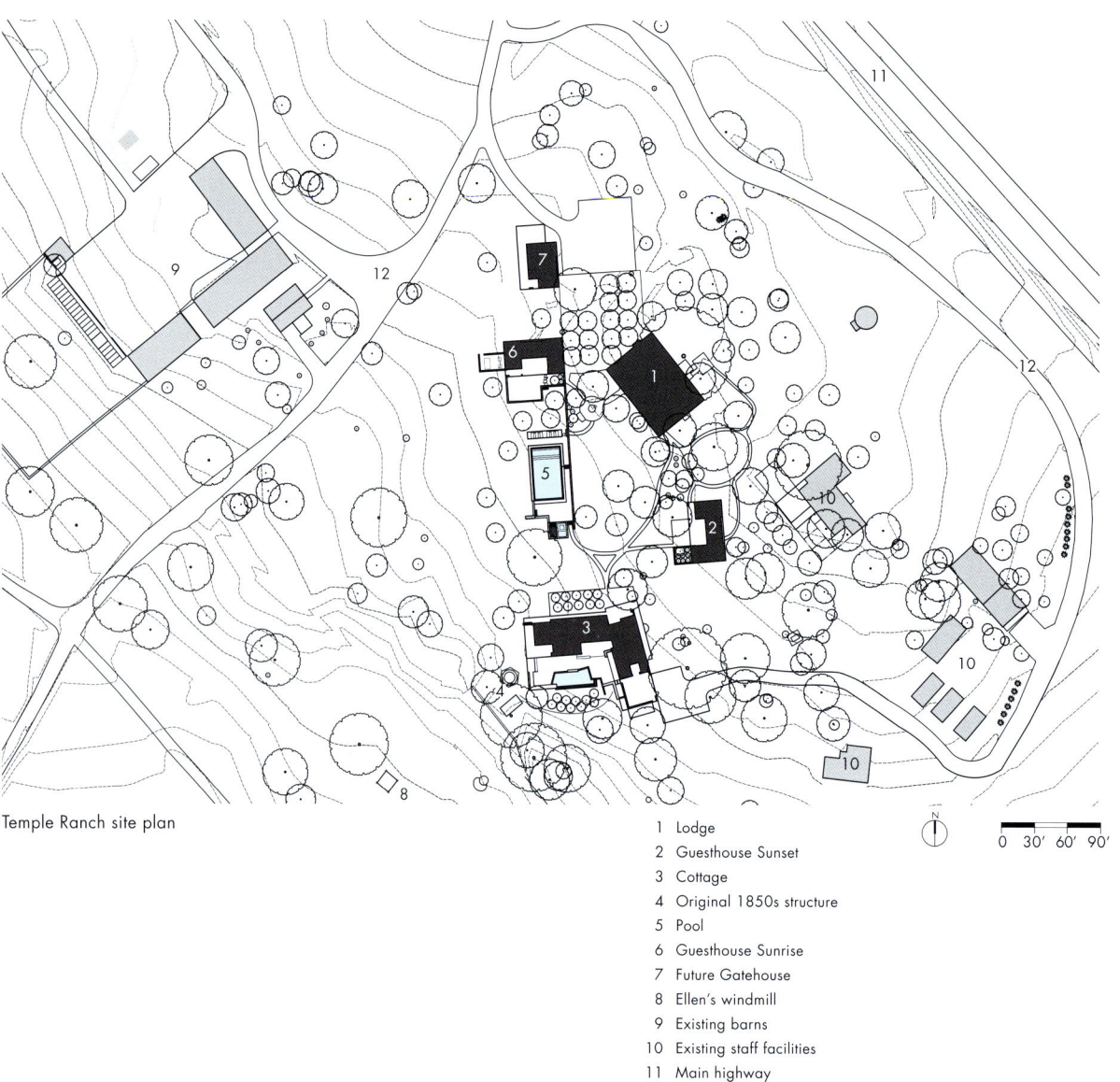

Temple Ranch site plan

1 Lodge
2 Guesthouse Sunset
3 Cottage
4 Original 1850s structure
5 Pool
6 Guesthouse Sunrise
7 Future Gatehouse
8 Ellen's windmill
9 Existing barns
10 Existing staff facilities
11 Main highway
12 Ranch road

Guesthouse Sunrise (counterclockwise from top):
View looking north
West facade
View looking southeast

(counterclockwise from top):
Covered porch of Guesthouse Sunrise
Window to shower in Guesthouse Sunset on north facade
North facade and covered porch of Guesthouse Sunset

opposite:
Looking toward lodge from Guesthouse Sunrise covered porch

overleaf:
Window detail and view looking south from Guesthouse Sunrise

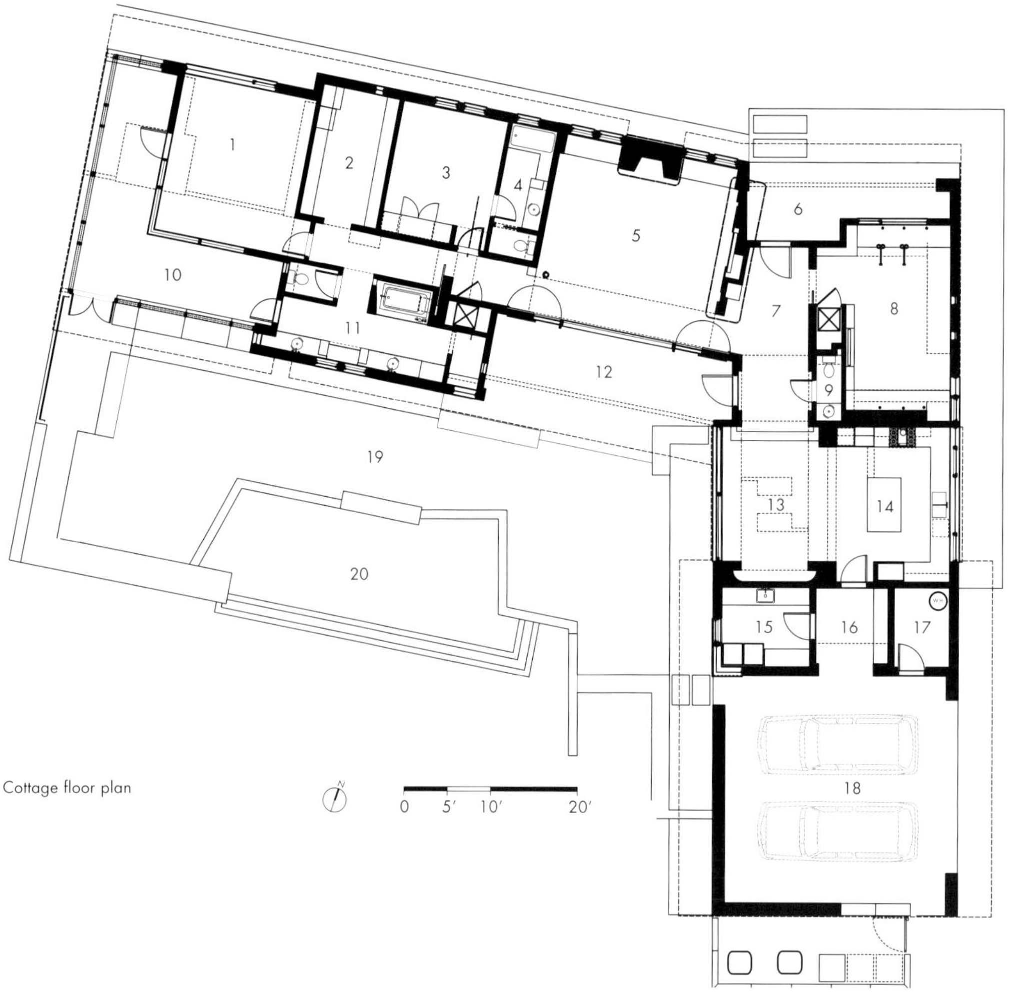

Cottage floor plan

1 Master bedroom
2 Master closet
3 Guest bedroom
4 Guest bathroom
5 Living room
6 Porch
7 Foyer
8 Office
9 Powder room
10 Screen porch
11 Master bathroom
12 Porch
13 Dining room
14 Kitchen
15 Laundry
16 Mud room
17 Mechnical
18 Carport
19 Terrace
20 Cooling pond

1 Bathroom
2 Bedroom
3 Living room
4 Bathroom
5 Bedroom
6 Porch

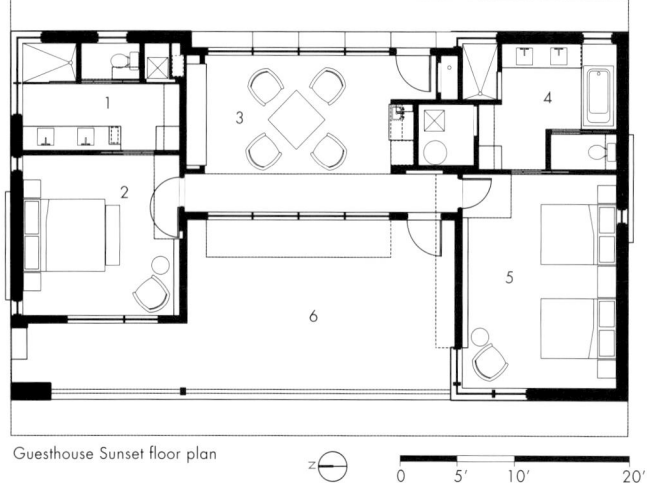

Guesthouse Sunset floor plan

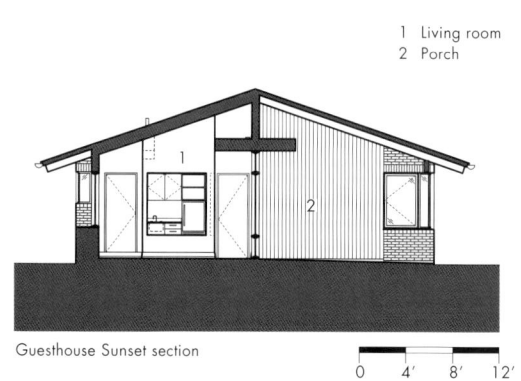

Guesthouse Sunset section

1 Living room
2 Porch

142  Natural Houses

Cottage carport

(counterclockwise from top):
Brick detail
Cottage window detail
Steel crosstie detail

opposite:
Cottage detail

overleaf:
Butterfly garden

Cottage (counterclockwise from top):
View looking southwest to pasture from living room
Entry sculpture shelf
Living room looking west to master bedroom

opposite:
View from master bedroom suite to entry

(counterclockwise from top):
View of Cottage from the southwest
Cottage interior screen porch
Temple Ranch at dusk

opposite:
Cottage kitchen

## Cabin on Flathead Lake

Outside Polson, Montana, 2007

Locals call the granite and shale cliff overlooking Montana's Flathead Lake "The Matterhorn." It is a place to observe the natural world: the lake, the surrounding ponderosa pine forest, and especially the eagles and ospreys that nest nearby. Together, the water, cliff, and trees form a classic picture of the expansive American West, and it is clear why Montana is still known as North America's great destination.

Within this context, the Cabin's diaphanous volume is set on six steel piers delicately anchored to solid concrete foundation blocks set into the steep slope. Large, screened walls enclose a living area, which has an open floor plan and wooden slat floors that extend outside. Private amenities are sparse but not neglected: a small kitchen, bathroom, and shower allow guests to stay should the mood strike them.

The shape of the roof in profile evokes the shallow V of a bird riding an updraft. But the building defers to its setting with more than material and aesthetic gestures. Construction workers poured the foundations by hand; sawed boards off-site; and screwed and bolted boards and framing together so the sounds of hammers, mixer trucks, and power saws would not frighten the ospreys nesting nearby. Visitors must approach the Cabin on foot as the building site is several hundred yards down a dirt road at the base of the slope.

From the Cabin's interior, an enveloping palette of locally harvested wood frames views of the forest beyond. The Cabin has no heating or cooling system and running water is pumped to the structure from the lake below. When communing with nature is the purpose of a building, minimal impact allows for maximum effect.

View of north facade at night

(counterclockwise from top):
View of lake
View of west facade
View of north facade

View looking south

overleaf:
Entry

(clockwise from top):
Living deck
Window detail
View looking north from living deck

opposite:
Beam detail

overleaf:
View looking north

Living deck

1  Bridge
2  Bathroom
3  Outdoor shower
4  Bedroom
5  Kitchen
6  Living deck
7  Deck

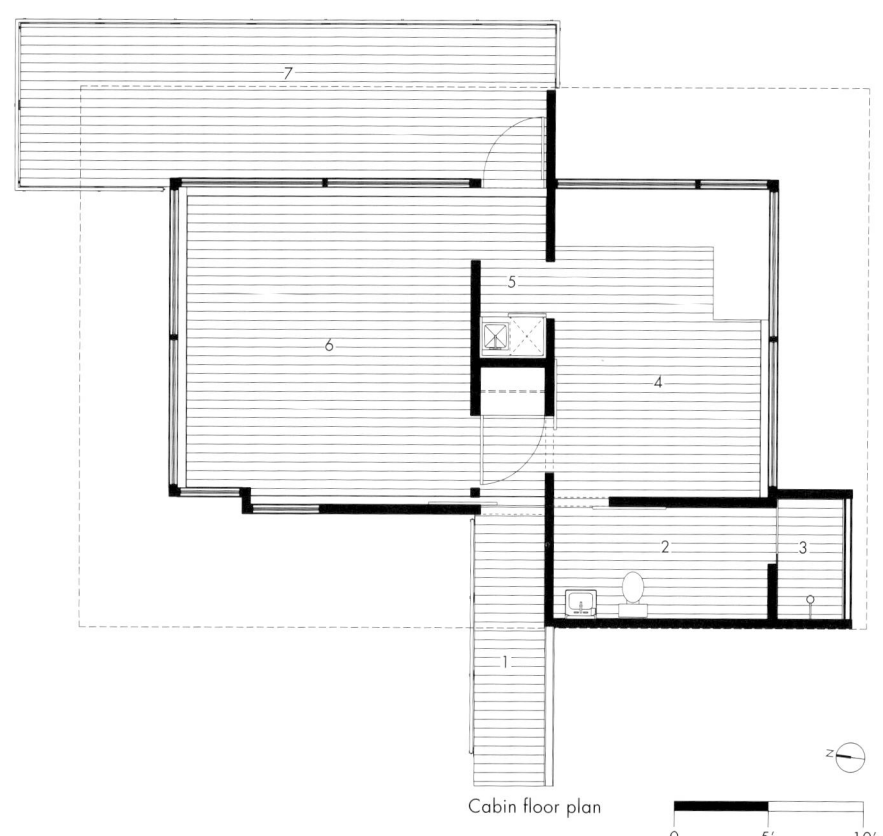

Cabin floor plan

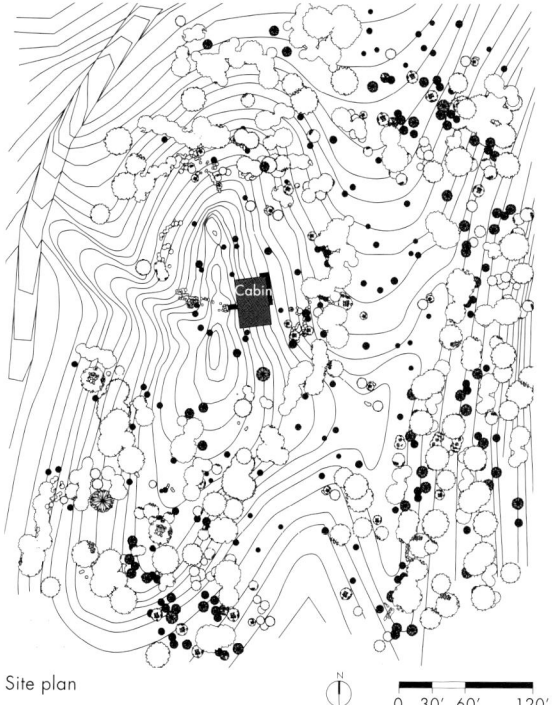

Site plan

1  Bedroom
2  Bathroom

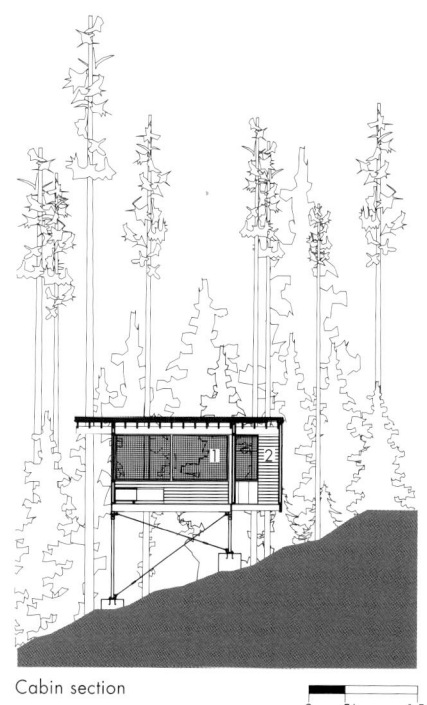

Cabin section

(left to right):
Bedroom and bathroom
Indoor/outdoor shower

opposite:
Entry detail

overleaf:
View of west facade

(counterclockwise from top):
View of west facade
Deck looking south
Deck looking north

opposite:
View from below at night

View of deck from below

(counterclockwise from top):
View of east facade from below
View of beam and osprey nest
Sunrise

overleaf:
View of lake

## Influential Texts

Appelton, Jay. *The Experience of Landscape.* London: Wiley, 1975.
Calvino, Italo. *Invisible Cities.* Italy: Giulio Einaudi Editore, 1972.
Emerson, Ralph Waldo. *Nature.* Published anonymously in 1836.
———. *Self-Reliance, Essays: First Series.* 1841.
Kant, Immanuel. *Observations on the Feeling of the Beautiful and Sublime.* Translated by John T. Goldthwait. Berkeley: University of California Press, 1961, 2003.
Nelson, Arthur C., Thomas W. Sanchez, and Casey J. Dawkins. *Urban Containment and Society.* Hampshire, UK: Ashgate, 2007.
Nelson, Arthur C., and Casey J. Dawkins. *Urban Containment in the United States.* Chicago: American Planning Association, 2004.
Pallasmaa, Juhani. *The Eyes of the Skin: Architecture and the Senses.* New York: John Wiley, 2005.
Roderick, Nash. *Wilderness and the American Mind.* New Haven, CT: Yale University Press, 1967.
Ruskin, John. *The Seven Lamps of Architecture.* New York: J. Wiley, 1849.
Schama, Simon. *Landscape and Memory.* New York: Random House of Canada, Limited, 1996.
Thoreau, Henry David. *Civil Disobedience, Resistance to Civil Government.* Aesthetic Papers, 1849.
———. *Walden; or, Life in the Woods.* Boston: Ticknor and Fields, 1854.
Vitruvius. *The Ten Books on Architecture.* Translated by Morris Hicky Morgan. Cambridge, MA: Harvard University Press, 1914.

## Illustration Credits

All images are the authors' unless otherwise indicated.

### Frontispiece
1, Art Gray
2, Paul Bardagjy
3, Art Gray
4, Matthew Millman
5–6, Art Gray

### Tower House
15–17, 19–25, 27–29, Art Gray

### Lake House
31–35, 37–39, 41–45, Paul Bardagjy

### Super Natural
51, 54, Art Gray

### House Above Lake Austin
59–63, Art Gray
64, Matthew Millman
65, Art Gray
66, Matthew Millman
67–71, 73, Art Gray
74, Matthew Millman
75, Art Gray

### Stone Creek Camp
77–81, 84–94, 96–97, 99–103, 105–107, Art Gray

### On the Salubrity of Sites
110, Art Gray
113, Matthew Millman

### Collector's House
117, Art Gray
118, Matthew Millman
119, Art Gray
121–23, 125 (top and bottom left), Matthew Millman
125 (bottom right), 126, Art Gray
127–29, Matthew Millman
130–31, Art Gray

### Temple Ranch
133–35, 137–41, 143–51, Art Gray

### Cabin on Flathead Lake
153–62, 164–73, Art Gray

## Project Team Credits

### Tower House
Kristen Heaney, Travis Greig

### Lake House
Jim Moore, Christopher Sanders

### House Above Lake Austin
Tim Dacey

### Stone Creek Camp
Christopher Sanders, Becky Joye, Matthew Ames

### Collector's House
Erlene Clark, Vincent Moccia

### Temple Ranch
Matthew Ames, Wenny Hsu, Christopher Sanders, Leland Ulmer

### Cabin on Flathead Lake
Jesse Coleman